Enter The Wu-Tang: How Nine Men Changed Hip-Hop Forever

By ALAN C. PAGE

Copyright © 2014 by Alan C. Page.

All rights reserved.

For information about permission to reproduce selections from this book, email alanpage@wutangbook.com

Cover design by DJ Underdog

About The Author photo taken by Amira Moore. Used by permission.

Published by Lone Gunman Media LLC.

Printed in the United States of America

ISBN-10: 0-692-20671-X
ISBN-13: 978-0-692-20671-3

http://wutangbook.com

DEDICATION

This book is dedicated to my wife, Amira, and my children, Amina and Khalil.

This book is also dedicated to my parents, who gave me my love for reading and always encouraged my writing.

Lastly, but never least, this book is dedicated to the memory of those who have returned to the essence: Ol' Dirty Bastard, Filli, Joy, Claude, and my grandfather, jazz trumpeter Oran "Hot Lips" Page. May you shine forever.

Chapter 1: Knowledge

On August 11, 1973, the man considered the founder of hip-hop, DJ Kool Herc, spun in public for the first time, at a Bronx party promoted by his sister, Cindy Campbell.[1] Twenty years later, hip-hop would take a quantum leap forward, when the Wu-Tang Clan struck hip-hop like a Category 5 hurricane on November 9, 1993, with the release of their debut album, *Enter The Wu-Tang (36 Chambers)* (*ETWT*). Dropping on the same day as A Tribe Called Quest's *Midnight Marauders* and a month after Black Moon's debut *Enta Da Stage*, the Clan combined the aggression of the latter with the commercial success of the former.[2]

Although East Coast acts such as Naughty by Nature, Onyx and Das Efx went platinum in this era, West Coast artists like Dr. Dre and Snoop Dogg were going *multi*-platinum.[3] Furthermore, even when artists were signed to the same label, less critically acclaimed West Coast acts went gold while their more critically acclaimed East Coast labelmates rarely reached that same sales level.[4] The momentum of hip-hop—from a sales perspective—appeared to have shifted west, 3,000 miles from where the genre started.

However, the commercial success of the Wu-Tang Clan, with their unapologetically East Coast hardcore rap style, reinvigorated the New York rap scene. The Clan's effect on New York radio played a major part in this reinvigoration. In the months leading up to the release of *ETWT*, now-legendary New York radio station Hot 97 would begin playing hip-hop in regular rotation for the first time, starting with *ETWT*'s breakout single "Method Man."[5] By reigniting excitement for the classic East Coast hardcore sound and kicking in the door for commercial airplay on a major local radio station, the Clan laid the perfect groundwork for two future icons to drop well-received debut albums the next year: The Notorious B.I.G. and Nas.[6] *The Village Voice* listed *ETWT*'s role in fueling New York rap's resurgence as the first reason why Wu-Tang Clan is the greatest rap group of all time.[7]

Commercial success for a hardcore rap album with minimal pop appeal is a rarity in the music world. This success could not have happened without a unique foundation upon which the success of the Wu-Tang Clan—and their debut album—was built. The foundation of the Wu begins almost thirty years before their debut album was even recorded.

If you mistook the Clan as merely a wild-eyed, testosterone soaked rap collective, you would never think to trace the ideology of the group to one former member of the Nation of Islam (NOI). In 1964, soon after Malcolm X's decision to leave the NOI sharply divided the members of Harlem's Mosque No. 7, Clarence 13X (later known as Father Allah) left the Nation of Islam and created The Nation of Gods and

Earths (NGE).[8] Up until Father Allah's exit from the NOI, the teachings of The Honorable Elijah Muhammad were known only to NOI members, but Father Allah began spreading these teachings, in a distilled form known as the 120 Lessons, throughout Harlem.[9]

In addition to the 120 Lessons, Father Allah taught two other sets of facts: The Supreme Alphabet (which correlated each of the twenty six letters of the Latin alphabet with a divine concept) and The Supreme Mathematics (which correlated the Arabic numerals 0-9 with ten concepts). The foundation of Allah's scientific system was the idea that every black man is God. The appeal of that idea to disenfranchised young black males cannot be overstated. This appeal helped the NGE ideology spread like wildfire.

Eventually, Father Allah opened a school, Allah School, near the intersection of 7th Avenue and 125th Street.[10] Allah School was opened with the assistance of both the Urban League and then-New York City mayor John Lindsay (who saw Father Allah as a figure who could positively impact Harlem's youth).[11] Allah's teachings would later profoundly influence hip-hop as a whole, following the introduction of NGE adherent Rakim (of iconic duo Eric B. & Rakim) to the world of music. The impact of NGE on global culture would not end there, however, as Father Allah's teachings would go on to deeply influence the nine members of the Wu-Tang Clan: Rza (pronounced "Rizza" and serving as acronym for

Ruler Zig-Zag-Zig Allah[12] in The Supreme Alphabet), Gza (pronounced "Jizza"[13] and signifying God Zig-Zag-Zig Allah in the Supreme Alphabet), Ol' Dirty Bastard, Inspectah Deck, Method Man, Ghostface Killah,[14] Raekwon, Masta Killa, and U-God.

In the beginning, however, there were only two: Rza and Ghostface Killah (often called simply "Ghost"), both of whom lived in the rough and tumble Stapleton Houses. Rza is often credited as the mastermind of the Wu, but Ghost arguably could share credit with Rza for the formation of the group, as a result of three crucial contributions.

First, Rza himself credits Ghost with being the first member of the Clan to come up with the idea of referring to himself as Wu-Tang, noting, "Ghost was the first one to say 'That's Wu-Tang, I'm Wu-Tang'."[15] Furthermore, Ghost claimed in a recent interview that he brought Rza the idea of using Wu-Tang—the name of one of the two clans of fighters in the film *Shaolin & Wu Tang*—as a group name.[16] In any case, both men likely share credit for convincing the other seven members to adopt the name.

The next crucial step in the formation of the group happened when Ghost and Rza put up the money to finance the recording of the first song recorded under the Wu-Tang Clan banner, "After The Laughter Comes Tears."[17] Rza and Ghost were the only Clan members featured on this first Wu-Tang recording. Finally, both men would combine their money to press up vinyl copies of "After The Laughter Comes Tears," Wu-Tang Clan's debut single.

However, "After The Laughter Comes Tears" was largely overshadowed by the A-side on the single, "Protect Ya Neck," which featured eight members of the Clan (everyone except Masta Killa, who declined Gza's invitation to the studio, on the day that wound up being the "Protect Ya Neck" recording session, to avoid missing school).[18] Whether by design or an accident of fate (and thanks to a short contribution from U-God that would generally be considered a bridge, not a verse), the presence of seven verses on this iconic song also fits neatly with NGE philosophy, since the number seven signifies god in the NGE's Supreme Mathematics numerical system (god, to them, being synonymous with black men).

After their independently released 12 inch vinyl single, "Protect Ya Neck" b/w "After The Laughter Comes Tears,"[19] sold thousands of copies, the Wu attracted the attention of several labels. However, Loud Records was the only label to accept Rza's demand that the Clan be signed without a "leaving member" clause—a standard record contract clause which required members of any signed group to release solo efforts on the same label to which the group was signed.[20] Foregoing deals from labels offering larger advances, the Clan signed to Loud, viewing the option to sign multiple lucrative solo deals at other labels as more valuable than a bigger upfront payday without that option.[21]

There are almost as many variations on the story of how the single was financed as there are Clan members on the track. Rza, U-God, Method Man, and Yoram Vazan (the owner of the recording studio where the single was recorded) all recall an entirely different set of circumstances relating to who paid for what. Rza recalls splitting the costs for the session with Ghost, which included paying for any Wu member who couldn't cover their share ($50 each).[22] U-God claims that he paid for the entire session himself.[23] Method Man recalls every Wu member contributing $100 (not $50).[24] Yoram Vazan, the studio owner, recalls the Clan not having enough money to pay for the session at all![25] No matter who actually paid what to record the Wu's independent single, once it was released, it became a resounding success.

Although it is generally agreed that the sales of "Protect Ya Neck" b/w "After The Laughter" were phenomenal for an independently released vinyl 12 inch, the exact number of units the single sold has never been established, with some sources claiming the single sold 10,000 copies (without citing sources),[26] while Rza himself has stated that the single sold even more (without citing a specific number).[27] It appears that only 10,000 copies of "Protect Ya Neck" b/w "After The Laughter" were manufactured[28] and they were not all sold. In fact, Wu associate Michael McDonald (a/k/a LASK) convinced his friend Sincere Thompson (then employed at Polygram) to mail scores of "Protect Ya Neck"/"After The Laughter" 12 inches to DJs, tastemakers and retail owners on Polygram's mailing list.[29]

Even though the Clan was not able to sell the pieces of vinyl sent through the Polygram mailing list, the resulting radio and in-store play their single received from the list recipients spread the furor over the Clan nationwide. Additionally, sending out the record in an official Polygram package gave the single more of a chance to be heard than if Rza or his three-man staff (Power, Mook and Divine) mailed the single to the power players on the Polygram list themselves.[30] The list included some of the most influential hip-hop radio DJs of that era, including Funkmaster Flex of Hot 97 and The Baka Boyz of Los Angeles' Power 106.[31] Most DJs who heard the record instantly loved it. Although exact sales numbers are unavailable, it is undisputed that the record went on to sell thousands of copies independently. The uproar caused by the single, bolstered by commercial mix show and college radio airplay, attracted multiple record labels that vied to sign the Clan. As mentioned earlier, the Clan chose to sign with Loud.

After the Clan signed their record deal, they made the decision to replace their independent single's B-side "After The Laughter

Comes Tears" with an explosive solo cut named after the emerging star in the group, Method Man, in order to re-release the single.[32] With Loud Records distribution, the re-released single took off, selling an average of one thousand copies a day in its first 30 days on the market.[33] An ad placed in *Billboard* touted the success of "Protect Ya Neck" b/w "Method Man", proudly boasting that the single had stayed on the rap charts for 25 consecutive weeks, a shocking success at the time for a hardcore hip-hop record.[34] Less constrained by corporate forces, college radio and commercial mix shows embraced the record and the Clan's single thrived on college stations and a growing number of hip-hop mix shows.

Mix shows aside, college radio was undeniably a huge source of early support for the Clan, particularly for the independent release of "Protect Ya Neck." Arguably as a nod to the early radio support for "Protect Ya Neck," Rza included interludes on *ETWT* sampling one of the Clan's early radio interviews and a clip of a Wu fan calling into a radio show to request that more Wu music be played.[35] The liner notes of *ETWT* also thank numerous college radio DJs who supported the Clan from the beginning. Furthermore, Michigan State University college radio personality Jason Staton is shouted out in the outro to "Wu-Tang Clan Ain't Nuthin' To F' Wit," as is *Gavin Report* college radio reporter Will Strickland. All the support from DJs around the country for both versions of the "Protect Ya

Neck" single—particularly the well-received "Method Man" B-side—laid the perfect groundwork for the November 9, 1993 release date Loud Records set for *ETWT*.

Great moments in hip-hop rarely happen in a vacuum. The release of *ETWT* is no exception, as that album was released on the same day as *Midnight Marauders*, the much-anticipated third album from A Tribe Called Quest (a group with a global appeal similar to the Clan, due to their fusion of jazz samples and Afrocentric motifs).[36] With two highly anticipated records hitting stores on the same day, hip-hop turnout in record stores on November 9th was virtually guaranteed. Furthermore, this would be a rematch of sorts between members of the Clan and Tribe, as Tribe frontman Q-Tip recently revealed that he battled Rza and Ol' Dirty Bastard back when he was in high school.[37]

However, the hip-hop climate in 1993 had changed greatly from the years when Rza and Ol' Dirty Bastard battled their way across New York City, which up until the late 1980s cast a long shadow across the rest of the world with its towering hip-hop output. By the time the Clan debuted, the commercial focus of hip-hop had shifted to California. Ironically, one longtime California resident whose video promotions work at Capitol Records aided that westward shift—-by securing MTV video airplay for popular West Coast singles "Bust A Move" (by Young MC) and "Wild Thing" (by Tone-Loc)—would be key in helping *ETWT* shift the balance back towards the East.[38] That longtime California resident is Loud Records founder, Steve Rifkind.

"Wu opened up the doors, I feel, for everybody," Rifkind said, looking back on the legacy of the Clan. "When Puff came [after us], the door was open. Hot 97 was a dance station. They didn't play any hip-hop. They just brought in [Funkmaster] Flex, to be a mixer, for mix show radio. They did like a 'Make It Or Break It'. First, it was 'Protect Ya Neck', but the record didn't do [anything]. Then once 'M-E-T-H-O-D' won eight days in a row and the results were ten to one [then the door was open for hip-hop to be played on Hot 97]."[39]

Rza viewed commercial success as important, but for a cultural purpose more vital than merely selling records. "When I first entered hip-hop, as an entrepreneur…I realized a lot of records were being sold all over the country…Hammer, Young MC, Tone Loc…East Coast wasn't making records that were selling…we had Tribe Called Quest, we had great artists and all that, but [there weren't] a lot of platinum artists," Rza reflected. "I felt like Wu-Tang was more of an awakening type of group, a group you're going to listen to and get something out of it, something you can tell your kids about. I felt like other artists can sell ten million records and there will still be ten million motherfuckers walking around buying Burger King and stupid. But if we could sell a million records, I thought there would be a million people who got a whole new enlightenment, new creativity, wisdom, [and] spirituality. I honestly believed that. That's why I injected what I injected into it. It will mean more—it doesn't have to be the biggest seller, but it'll mean more to the world. And I think it did. I think my idea was right and exact and it was a wise decision I made back then."[40]

When Rza spoke about giving his listeners a new type of wisdom, he was likely referring to the wisdom he acquired from a group to which he has belonged for most of his life: the Nation of Gods and Earths (NGE). NGE adherents often say "knowledge is one because knowledge is the foundation." To gain knowledge of NGE philosophy and martial arts films is to acquire deeper knowledge regarding the Clan's music, because NGE philosophy and martial arts film iconography are the foundation of the Clan's music.[41]

Even casual fans of the Wu who are unaware of the NGE's influence on the group are aware of the influence of Asian martial arts film on the Clan.[42] The first voice heard on *ETWT* is from *Shaolin & Wu-Tang*, a kung fu movie centered around Shaolin monks and a warrior from Wu-Tang Mountain, whose village was destroyed by government forces. Describing their style of rhyming as analogous to the Wu-Tang sword style and re-christening their home borough, Staten Island, as "Shaolin" added a level of mysticism to Wu that separated them from every other hardcore rap crew.

The kung fu film influence on the Wu harkens back to their childhoods. As elementary school students, Rza and Ol' Dirty Bastard would trek to Times Square to watch double and sometimes triple features of kung fu films, when that genre was near the height of its popularity.[43] "In 1979, my cousin [Dirty] took me to 42nd Street to see some kung fu movies and I was blown away," Rza recalled, in one interview. "We started going every weekend after that."[44]

These childhood experiences between Wu members are essential to note because their brotherly bond is the central component upon which the strength of the Wu is built. This bond exists because many of the group's members have long histories with one another that pre-date the formation of the Clan. Gza, Raekwon and Inspectah Deck have known each other since elementary school.[45] Method Man and U-God made music together before the Clan formed (and also grew up in the Park Hill Apartments, as did Raekwon and Inspectah Deck).[46] Rza and Ghostface Killah grew up in Stapleton Houses. Before Wu-Tang Clan was assembled, Rza and two of his cousins—Gza and Ol' Dirty Bastard—formed an early group called All In Together Now, which gained some early buzz long before the Clan formed.[47]

Wu members even taught one another how to rhyme. "I started [in] hip-hop as an MC first, taught by the Gza," Rza revealed to one interviewer.[48]

The importance of Rza starting in hip-hop as an emcee might not initially appear noteworthy until that fact is viewed in light of how young Rza was when he first became involved in hip-hop production. He recalled in one interview that he began making music in elementary school. "I started getting into beats at eleven years old," Rza recounted in an interview with *Kotori Magazine*. "I had a beat machine that was just a rhythm box. You push one button, it says 'waltz'. The other says 'bossa nova', 'soul', 'rock', know what I mean? But if you push two buttons together, it creates a new sound."[49]

Although many commentators have overlooked Ol' Dirty Bastard's production prowess,[50] ODB actually began producing beats with Rza in this early period. "Me and Ol' Dirty made hundreds of [beat] tapes with that beat machine." Later, in the same interview, Rza revealed that his entrepreneurial bent dated all the way back to his childhood. "I had to sell newspapers to buy all my equipment back then," Rza recalled, then quickly added: "Or steal some."[51]

Still, most of Rza's equipment appeared to have been acquired legitimately, and at no small cost for an elementary school student, demonstrating an early (and unusual) fiscal discipline at a young age. "By the time I was twelve, I had saved up enough to buy the echo box, the mic, and that beat machine. That was a $100 beat machine."[52]

Rza's determination to invest monetarily in a music career from an early age is even more phenomenal when one considers the challenges the Clan faced as children. According to one source, Rza's mother didn't even have a bank account until after the Clan achieved commercial success.[53] "Your bed was whatever spot you could grab on the floor," Rza wrote in his book *The Tao of Wu*, when reflecting on his impoverished upbringing in a two-bedroom apartment shared by *nineteen* people.[54] In another example of difficulties Clan members faced even in childhood, Inspectah Deck's father died when he was six.[55] Ghostface's father left his household when he was the same age.

"My father left me when I was 6," Ghostface recalled in a 1997 interview. "My mother tried to take care of all of us on public assistance."[56] In the same interview, U-God mentions that he also grew up without a father in his life.

These early struggles seemed to seal the bond between the Clan's members tighter than one might usually find in a rap group. "I never jumped from crew to crew. I always stayed with cats that—even to this day, that I have thirty year relationships with," Raekwon recounted, speaking on the importance of personal history between the group members. "We never had fathers, all we had was each other."[57]

"We showed what you could do if you brought your minds together. You can do anything in the world, baby," Method Man declared.[58]

Chapter 2: Wisdom

When the Clan started, they relied on the strength and wisdom of two men: Rza and Gza. The two cousins acquired that wisdom as a result of the experiences they had as the first members of the Clan to successfully acquire solo record deals, before the group itself officially formed. At the time he landed his solo deal, Rza was going by the name Prince Rakeem. He was signed to Tommy Boy Records, which had recently released *3 Feet High and Rising*, the debut album from De La Soul. Gza was known as The Genius (an alter ego he has kept throughout his career). He was signed to Cold Chillin' Records, home to highly popular NGE hip-hop artist Big Daddy Kane.

As Prince Rakeem, Rza would release a single called "Ooh I Love You, Rakeem" that represented an artistic compromise between his traditional rugged style and the formulaic rap single format then deemed most likely to be successful at radio. The lead single to The Genius' *Words From The Genius*, "Come Do Me," was also an artistic compromise, made in an attempt to craft the ever-elusive "radio friendly" record. Both efforts failed; Rza and Gza found themselves back at square one: unsigned and underground once again.[59]

When Rza began assembling the Clan, it seems that he gained two valuable lessons from the challenges he and Gza faced early in their solo careers. First, Rza learned that attempting to imitate the formulas of other acts was unlikely to lead to success. Instead, Rza, Gza, and the rest of the Clan would develop their own unique aggressive style, a style likely formed as a result of the group's tradition of engaging in intense intra-group battling (akin to martial artists sparring to sharpen their combat readiness).[60]

This aggressive style would distinguish the Clan from other rap contemporaries who enjoyed commercial success in 1993, a time when rappers usually attained major sales only after they softened their sound to secure commercial radio play, at least for their singles. "[Wu-Tang] proved, more than anything, that you could sell a shitload of records without tons of radio play," Rifkind said, reflecting on *ETWT* years later.[61]

The Clan tradition of battling possibly derived from Rza and Dirty's history of battling rappers across New York City, years before the Clan was even formed. "Early on, Ol' Dirty Bastard and I used to watch kung fu movies, leave the theater, do some kung fu fighting, get on the train, keep fighting, and then run into MCs and musically battle them like it was a kung fu fight," Rza reflected.[62]

The aggressive lyrical styles that originated from the Clan's background in battling made the resulting first record featuring most of the Clan, "Protect Ya Neck," the audio equivalent of a blood-soaked kung fu epic: dramatic, highly charged and loaded with testosterone. The heavily male underground rap audience of the early 90s ate it up. It was a summer blockbuster for your stereo.

The second lesson Rza learned from the failure of his solo debut single was that he could not rely on others to market his music. As such, Rza concluded that the Wu should release their first group project independently, following his unsavory experience at Tommy Boy Records. Rza did not arrive at this conclusion without careful consideration. Even after the label botched the promotion of his single, Rza briefly considered approaching Tommy Boy about signing the Wu-Tang Clan, before his deal there fell apart. However, Rza changed his mind about that when he encountered legal trouble in the small Ohio town of Steubenville and Tommy Boy did not provide him with any assistance.[63] After this experience, Rza realized that he should take the fate of his brothers in his own hands and put out their music himself.

The decision to independently release "Protect Ya Neck" b/w "After The Laughter" (and the ensuing success of the single on an indie level) would allow Rza to approach labels from a position of strength, as he negotiated the group deal for Wu-Tang Clan. A mini-bidding war broke out between labels vying to sign them, stoked by the group's then-unprecedented feat of selling thousands of copies of their single independently. When the smoke cleared, the Clan decided to sign with the then unknown Loud Records, founded by a man named Steve Rifkind, who had gained notoriety by convincing major labels to underwrite the audacious method of promotion known as "street teaming."[64] It was to be a match made in heaven between two promotional visionaries: Rifkind and Rza.

"I will never forget that day," Rifkind said, describing the moment he decided to sign the Clan, after watching all nine members perform live in his Loud office. "There were nine guys in a group that could spit their asses off. When I saw them, I thought they could be as big as the Rolling Stones."[65]

Rifkind's confidence in the group's commercial viability was likely a key reason why he was willing to accept demands from Rza that other labels would not. Scores of rap groups before the Clan had signed record contracts containing "leaving member" clauses, under which record labels reserved the right to release solo records that any member of a contractually bound group wanted to release. The key point Rza secured when negotiating with Loud was making sure that the Wu's contract did not include a "leaving member" clause, so Wu-Tang Productions had the option to secure Wu solo deals at other labels. Once multiple solo deals were signed, several different labels had a vested interest in the success of the Wu-Tang Clan as a whole (since each label who signed a Wu member to a solo deal knew that successful sales from any

Wu-related album would make it easier to market the solo Wu artist signed to their respective label).

After Rza and Gza had attempted to launch solo careers without the strength in numbers inherent in the Clan, Rza had (perhaps inadvertently) learned the importance of cross-branding. As a result of gaining this valuable wisdom, Rza made sure the first wave of Wu solo projects all featured the iconic Wu-Tang Clan logo as part of their artwork, no matter what label distributed the project.

Rza's brother, Mitchell "Divine" Diggs—who has played a long running role in managing the business affairs of the Clan—also saw the importance of Rza's plan to assure individual Clan members retained the right to sign to other labels. "We had an understanding that the number of people in our band couldn't survive under one small [recording] fund," Divine reflected when asked about the historic deal by a *Time* interviewer in 2000. "You have to create something that would be able to grow financially and create stability for all. We basically felt that if we could have the individuals go out and pursue their own careers that one's success wouldn't destroy the others. And when one rises, it rises the flag of Wu, instead of saying 'Hey, Wu may break up because they can't split $100,000'. We learned that and we applied [that wisdom] and I think the guys in the band are grateful to us for thinking that way, because now they can have their own individual budgets and, when it's time to come back together, they can share a huge pot."[66]

However, at the time the deal with Loud was being discussed, the prospect of these solo deals was not necessarily a guarantee. Loud's proposed deal offered the least financial incentive of all the deals on the table that Wu was considering.[67] Accepting the deal with Loud showed how the group trusted Rza with their future, even if it meant accepting less money in the present moment. In an interview almost twenty years after the negotiations concluded, Ghostface recalled that although Loud offered the least upfront money of all the deals on the table, the group considered the Loud deal the most favorable, because Loud acquiesced to Rza's demand that Wu members have the option to seek solo deals elsewhere.[68]

One cannot fully appreciate the Clan's foresight in agreeing to forego offers with larger upfront advances, unless one understands the financial hardship the Clan endured while the deal was being negotiated. "Meth told me back then he was living like a Viking, no hot water, no heat!" *ETWT* album engineer Ethan Ryman recalled, selecting that specific example to illustrate his amazement that the Clan turned down deals with more upfront money at a time when they were all struggling monetarily.[69]

There was one other important concession that Rifkind (and Loud) granted to the

Clan in their contract negotiation: creative control—the Wu would be able to record their music as they saw fit.[70]

This last concession was key to allowing the group to bring their visionary album to the masses their way, untouched by corporate interference.

Before there was an actual Wu-Tang Clan, Rza created the production company to which they would be signed: Wu-Tang Productions. "So we had the name, but we still didn't have a group," Rza humorously recalled in *The Wu-Tang Manual*. "It's funny, you see that later with the dot-com companies, claiming domain names before they even have a company."[71]

Clan members believed in Rza from the very beginning. Speaking about the importance of Rza in an interview, Raekwon explained, "We believed in him…he was the general. He was the Phil Jackson. Because we already saw how he [had] achieved something, getting a record done on his own. Remember, the Gza and Rza had a deal back then [before *ETWT*]. We were still in the street. They came back to the block with album covers. Those were like trophies. [Rza] was so smart. He had knowledge of self. He was a respectable brother. We said, 'we believe [in] you, we're willing to let you sit in the driver's seat.'"[72]

The faith Rza engendered expanded beyond the Clan, to everyone who participated in the making of their debut album. Yoram Vazan, owner of Firehouse Studios (the tiny 1,000 square foot Brooklyn studio[73] where *ETWT* was recorded) recalled the breadth of Rza's vision and his confidence when he recounted a conversation with Rza about the number of albums Rza planned to record there, in addition to *ETWT*. "I remember RZA came in and said, 'I got six albums to do with you'," Vazan recalled. "It was [the] Wu-Tang [debut album], Method Man, ODB, Gravediggaz, and I think he did two more at the same time. They couldn't afford to pay, but RZA said, 'Don't worry, we're gonna pay you back.' He was there for six months. They made Firehouse their home."[74]

In a separate interview, Vazan recalled that the Clan didn't even have enough money to pay for the recording session for "Protect Ya Neck," a song that made a powerful impression on Vazan. "It was an amazing track, very wild and hardcore," Vazan recalled. "I used to walk in and out of the room and hang out and listen to the stuff, but when they finished they didn't have enough money to pay! I told RZA, 'Don't worry about it, man, give me it when you have it.'"[75] Rza's faith was almost infectious in that way, convincing Vazan, a complete stranger to Rza, to allow the Clan to record in his studio, even when they had no money to pay for all the studio time they used.

Vazan wasn't the only person at Firehouse who acted in accordance with Rza's vision. Engineers who worked with Rza at the time *ETWT* was recorded noted that Rza had a very specific idea of how he wanted the record to sound. "Rakeem doesn't want too much high gloss in his record," said Ethan Ryman, an engineer at Firehouse at the time, who engineered the majority of the album. "He wants it to sound clear, but he also wants it to sound like a basement tape, almost. You'll hear a lot of rough stuff [musically], but their voices are much clearer than most rap releases I've heard."[76]

However, Rza's uncanny confidence in his sonic vision was not shared by everyone who worked at the Clan's record label. *ETWT* mastering engineer Chris Gehringer recalled several unnamed Loud executives who were concerned about the sound quality of the final mix of *ETWT*. "There were no real arguments from the group about the sound quality [of the album], but a lot of people at the label were like, 'Okay, that's it?'" Gehringer said. "I was like, 'Yeah, that's what they gave me. It's not going to really get any better sound-wise than that.'"[77]

Despite this handful of naysayers, the Clan had earned the unshakable confidence of the most important person at Loud: label head and founder Steve Rifkind. In an interview conducted while *ETWT* was being recorded, Rifkind was asked what the plan was for the Clan. "We need to have Wu-Tang Clan finish this album, so we can get it out and go platinum with it," Rifkind said, as if the success of the group was a foregone conclusion.[78] The forthright assurance in Rifkind's answer clearly demonstrates that Rza and the Clan had the full confidence of their label head, even in the early stages of recording their debut. That confidence in the commercial viability of the Clan appeared to be a self-fulfilling prophecy, as *ETWT* was certified gold by April of 1994, after selling half a million copies.[79] It was certified platinum on May 15, 1995, representing one million units shipped to retailers, roughly a year and a half after its debut.[80]

Rifkind's confidence was likely fueled by Rza's own self-assured vision for the group. Prince Paul, a DJ for Stetsasonic and a producer for De La Soul, explained how Rza's vision for the future of the Wu was long in the making. "He was telling me how he figured out how to manipulate the whole industry. 'I'm going to do this, and I'm going to put these records out, then get bigger deals…' and I was like 'Yeah, word'. But everything he said happened exactly how he figured it out."[81] Eventually, Rza would secure the type of record deal he described to Prince Paul, with the terms he mentioned, from Rifkind's label, Loud.

Rifkind agreed to these terms because he saw Rza's vision, which shows astounding foresight, since the confidence that the group had in themselves was not initially shared by all the record executives they encountered early in the group's career, even from executives who were steeped in hip-hop tradition. Bonz Malone, an A&R executive at Island at the time, who had extensive roots in hip-hop culture, recalled Rza bringing the "Protect Ya Neck" single to him to secure a record deal and admitted he did not grasp the commercial potential of the group or the concept behind their name. "When Rza brought 'Method Man' and 'Protect Ya Neck' to me—this was in '91, I already had signed Mobb Deep—I thought it was incredible, but I gotta be honest, I had no idea what them dudes was trying to do as well," Bonz reflected. "I remember laughing hard as hell. He told me about how Staten Island was Shaolin…and their ideology and all that. I remember telling him, 'Nigga, who the hell is gonna follow that?'"[82]

It should be noted, of course, that Rifkind was not the only record executive who saw the commercial potential of the Clan at this early stage in their career. Wu received offers from other companies, but Loud was the only company that conceded to *all* of Rza's demands, particularly Rza's insistence on Clan members being allowed to sign solo deals at other labels. Even as the group deal was being negotiated, interest in signing Wu members to solo deals grew rapidly, in one case even before the group's debut album was recorded.

Although "Method Man" was the song that brought Method Man's solo capabilities to the attention of many listeners, the Def Jam executive who signed Method Man to his solo deal, Tracy Waples, first saw his potential as a solo artist after listening to Meth's verse on the A-side of Wu's debut single. "I heard him [on] 'Protect Ya Neck', which was their first single. He had a real dope vocal performance on there. It just stood out a lot. When I met them, when I saw him in person, I said, 'He looks like a star, he's going to be a star'. So, we signed him here at Def Jam. Prince Rakeem—I call him the overseer—he just basically has a hand over the whole thing…I went out to Shaolin where they make all their music. We sat down and kicked it. Meth was with it [as far as signing to Def Jam]," said Waples.[83]

In the midst of handling various Wu-related negotiations, Rza was also strategic enough to get one of his more formally educated associates from Staten Island, Schott Free, a job at Loud, so he would have an executive on the inside of the label who had the Clan's best interest at heart. "[RZA] said, 'Look man, you one of the only educated dudes in the Clan. We need somebody up in the office, overseeing what these guys are doing with our records!'" Schott Free recalled.[84] Free was no record industry novice; he had prior experience servicing the "Protect Ya Neck" single to radio stations around the country. As a testament to the good name Free had built for himself while servicing "Protect Ya Neck," one of the DJs he serviced with that single—an influential underground DJ named Stretch Armstrong—also lobbied Loud head Rifkind to hire Free as an A&R there, which Rifkind eventually did. Needless to say, Free was then (and remains) one of the most enthusiastic supporters of the Clan.

Nonetheless, the most enthusiastic supporters of the Clan's music were the group themselves. They had an unflagging confidence that their music would be not just successful, but paradigm-shifting for their genre as a whole. "We gonna rock the industry. We gonna fuck everybody up," Ol' Dirty Bastard bragged during one early interview while *ETWT* was being recorded.[85]

Even when acknowledging the long odds against their success, as a group from a very underrepresented New York borough, Clan members expressed a deep assurance that they could still beat those odds. "We was always last," Ghostface recalled. "You had Brooklyn, Manhattan, [and other boroughs that had successful rap acts before Staten Island did]…but like they always say, 'The first shall be last and the last shall be first.'"[86]

It could be argued that the clarity of Rza's visionary plan for the group played a key role in their confidence that they would succeed. Part of Rza's vision for the album involved incorporating the iconic martial arts films the Clan enjoyed as children into the album's overall soundscape. The three martial arts films most influential to the Clan generally, and influential to the recording of *ETWT* specifically, were released in the late 70s and early 80s: *The 36th Chamber of Shaolin*[87] (1978), *Mystery of Chessboxing* (or *Ninja Checkmate*)[88] (1979), and *Shaolin & Wu Tang* (also called *Shaolin versus Wu Tang*) (1983).[89]

These films are the source of the names of the group itself and several of its members. The group name Wu-Tang Clan is derived from *Shaolin & Wu Tang*. Ghostface Killah[90] derived his name from the villain in the film *Mystery of Chessboxing* (a song on *ETWT* also shares this film's title). The protagonist in *The 36th Chamber of Shaolin* is named Master Killer (from whom Wu member Masta Killa probably derives his name). The decision to assign Raekwon The Chef the "chef" part of his stage name was partially influenced by a character featured in *Mystery of Chessboxing*. "[I]n a bunch of the original Wu-Tang movies, one of the best fighters was this character named The Chef. The guy who played him was named Yuen Siu Tien…he had a pudgy look about him, like Raekwon. So that's another reason we call him the Chef," Rza recalled.[91] Lastly, the Clan decided to re-christen their home borough, Staten Island, as Shaolin, the name of a temple of kung fu practicing monks featured in several films, but perhaps most famously in *Shaolin & Wu-Tang*.

"Shaolin shadowboxing and the Wu-Tang sword style. If what you say is true, the Shaolin and the Wu-Tang could be dangerous," "Do you think your Wu-Tang sword can defeat me," and "En garde, I'll let you try my Wu-Tang style" are the three martial arts film vocal samples that open the album, prefacing the opening track, "Bring Da Ruckus." The first two vocal samples are derived from Gordon Liu's classic 1983 film *Shaolin & Wu-Tang*,[92] the film from which much of the Clan's iconic mythology is derived, including the group's name. The third vocal sample from the album's opening, "En garde, I'll let you try my Wu-Tang style," is derived from the 1980 Shaw Brothers feature *Ten Tigers from Kwangtung* and refers to the Wu-Tang sword style.[93]

"En garde" is a warning that is traditionally exchanged between swordfighters to be prepared (on guard) before combat begins.[94] The usage of the metaphor of swords to represent the verbal dexterity of the Clan goes all the way back to the first single released by the group, on "Method Man" (where Meth describes a fictional Wu opponent's defeat by saying "Another corn chopped by the Wu-Tang sword").

Metaphors paralleling the sharpness of swords with lyrical dexterity (sharpness of wit) also recur throughout *ETWT*. The first sharpness metaphor on *ETWT* appears on the album's second track, "Shame on a Nigga," as Method Man brags that his style is "razor sharp" enough to "sever the head from the shoulders" of his competitors. On the second verse of *ETWT*'s third track, "Clan In Da Front," Gza boasts, "I come sharp as a blade and I cut you slow."

On the album's fourth track, in the fifth verse of "Wu-Tang: 7th Chamber," Rza warns potential musical competition that he's "quick to stick a Wu-Tang sword, straight through your navel." Masta Killa's closing verse in "Da Mystery of Chessboxin" (the album's fifth track) contains a line where he brags that his flow "stabs you like a dagger." "Chessboxin" also starts with a vocal sample from *Shaolin & Wu-Tang* stating "the game of chess is like a swordfight," bringing chess into the album's extended swordplay theme.

Being "sharp" is a long-used slang term for intelligence, cunning or skill.[95] Perhaps following this tradition of using sharpness as a metaphor for technical skill, Rza and other Clan members often contrast the Wu Tang sword style with their own vocal prowess at rapping.

"The thing about Wu-Tang in their films is their sword style, how they used the sword. We took the idea that our tongue is our sword and the best sword style is the Wu-Tang sword [style]," Rza reflected. "I always told the group, 'We're the Wu-Tang Clan. We've got the best lyric[al] style. Trust me, nobody can fuck with us. And with our sword, we're going to cut everybody's head[s] off.' That's why our first song was called 'Protect Ya Neck.'"[96]

On "Wu-Tang Clan Ain't Nuthin' To F' Wit," Method Man breaks down Rza's name as "short for razor." In an interview segment later in the album where Method Man explains the meanings behind each Clan members' name, Meth expounds on the idea of Rza being synonymous with a razor by explaining that Rza is "the sharpest motherfucker in the whole Clan, he['s] always on point, razor sharp, with the beats, with the rhymes, *and* he DJ[s]."

When Rza adapted his current stage name (perhaps to distinguish his work with the Clan from his solo career as Prince Rakeem), he inadvertently inspired the Genius to create a parallel identity: The Gza. In a bonus interview on the *Wu: The Story of Wu-Tang* DVD, Raekwon explained that the Rza's name was a play on the word razor, then recounted how Genius changed his name to Gza to parallel Rza's post-Prince Rakeem name change, a parallel seen as necessary since they were "both the ambassadors to the crew, our older brothers."

This parallel between names was apt, because Rza and Gza often seemed to be of one mind. For example, both Rza and Gza were remarkably consistent in how they compared swordsmanship to the Clan's music. "Wu-Tang also represents the sword style of rhyming. Being that we're lyrical or verbal assassins, we're fully aware that the tongue is symbolic to the sword," said Gza in an interview with iconic rap video show *Yo! MTV Raps*.[97]

The theme of verbal combat and using words as weapons is especially present in *ETWT's* sampled intro and its opening track, "Bring Da Ruckus."[98] The very first words heard on the album are a vocal sample referencing "Shaolin shadowboxing and the Wu-Tang sword style," while the next vocal sample explains how the Wu-Tang style can be dangerous. On the opening line of "Bring Da Ruckus," Ghostface Killah threatens competitors that they can "catch the blast of" (i.e. be shot by) "a hype verse," later describing his "P.L.O. style" as "dangerous," paralleling his rap style with a then-infamous terrorist group to emphasize the lethal nature of his rap abilities.[99] In the next verse, Raekwon compares the danger presented by the Clan to their competition as similar to "forty Macs."[100] Inspectah Deck follows, threatening that his "Wu-Tang slang'll leave your headpiece hanging" (i.e. knock off part of your scalp), bragging that he "verbally assault[s] with the tongue" and claiming that his "style shocks ya knot like the stun gun." ("knot" being slang for "head"). Gza is even more direct, saying simply "My Wu-Tang slang is mad fucking dangerous" and "more deadly than the stroke of an ax." And this is all in the first four verses on the record!

The theme of paralleling the verbal aggressiveness of battle rap with physical carnage continues throughout *ETWT*. On the third track, "Clan In Da Front," Gza threatens an imaginary foe that he'll "hang your ass with this microphone

[cord]." In the third verse of "Wu-Tang: 7th Chamber," Inspectah Deck reveals that even music itself is unsafe from the Clan's verbal assault, boasting that he was "charged by the system, for murdering the rhythm."

Rza's intro for "Clan In Da Front" continues the theme of the Clan's styles being lethal when he describes those styles as "36 chambers of death." "36 chambers" is a reference to the martial arts film classic *The Thirty Sixth Chamber of Shaolin*, which tells the story of a young man—whose village was destroyed by his government for rebelling—who seeks to master the thirty-five different styles of Shaolin fighting (each style being described as a chamber), to avenge his village.[101] He is kicked out of the temple before he is able to complete his training, but gains his revenge, then returns triumphantly to the temple, where he eventually develops a thirty-sixth style (the 36th chamber), which is a style designed to be easily accessible to laypeople.[102]

"36 chambers of death" is not the only reference on *ETWT* to martial arts styles utilized in the Clan's favorite films. On "Shame On A Nigga," Ol' Dirty Bastard describes his style as "tiger verse crane," two wildly different styles of kung fu featured in several films that influenced the Clan.[103] "Da Mystery of Chessboxin" opens with two vocal samples, the second of which ["The toad style is immensely strong and immune to nearly any weapon. When it's properly used, it's almost invincible"] is another *ETWT* reference to a particular martial arts style, the toad style, which was used most famously in the 1978 film *Five Deadly Venoms* (from which the sample originates).[104]

"That's how I felt Wu was, 'when properly used, it's almost invincible'. When [our style is] *properly* used, [we're almost invincible,]" Rza said, in an interview with *Wired*.[105]

With Rza's wisdom, he guided the Clan towards using their styles properly.

Chapter 3: Understanding

While Rza played the key role in making *ETWT* a beloved album from a musical perspective, it was Method Man who (by and large) played the key role in making Wu-Tang accessible from the vocal side, particularly with his knack for hooks. In one interview, Rifkind contrasted the ordinary crowd reaction when one DJ played "Protect Ya Neck" with the sheer pandemonium that broke out on the dance floor when the same DJ played "Method Man."[106] He went on to describe this as the moment when he knew the Clan was onto something special. This anecdote is no isolated incident, as it is generally accepted that Meth's star appeal was key to helping the Clan reach a broader audience than they might otherwise have reached without him.[107]

Unlike most of the Clan, Method Man spent part of his upbringing in a suburban area, specifically Long Island, which he described as markedly different from "dismal" life in the Park Hill Apartments.[108] Interacting with people from divergent walks of life likely helped Method Man foster his uncanny ability to incorporate pop culture references into his lyrics that appeal to a diverse range of people, since he saw from an early age which pop culture references resonated across starkly different communities.[109]

Meth's gift for creating widely accessible songs by weaving together disparate pop culture references is best exemplified on "Method Man." Released August 3, 1993, "Method Man" is a veritable pop culture potpourri, incorporating elements going back a full three centuries before the song was recorded.[110] The opening line in the song ("Hey, you, get off of my cloud") is a quote from the hook to The Rolling Stones' 1965 song "Get Off of My Cloud," which predates "Method Man" by almost 30 years.[111] "Cloud" was the second international number one record for the Stones and (along with their first international hit "Satisfaction") established that the Stones were not just a cover band re-doing hits by black artists (as their debut album, filled with covers, led some of their detractors to believe). It is ironic that the song that established the originality of a band that had been criticized by some for relying too often on covering black music would later provide the first line, on the first hit, from a group viewed as a cornerstone of a major black musical genre.

The next reference in "Method Man" is over three centuries old. "Pat a cake, pat a cake, hey, the Method Man" references the English traditional folk song "Pat-a-Cake, Pat-a-Cake, Baker's Man," which first appeared in print in Thomas D'Urfey's 1698 play, *The Campaigners.*[112] Continuing the multicultural blitzkrieg, another reference comes immediately after that line ("Sam I am and I don't eat green eggs and ham"), a homage to Dr. Seuss' 1960 work *Green Eggs and*

Ham,[113] with a nod to the prohibition against eating pork in NGE teachings.[114] To illustrate the cultural potency of the references selected by Method Man, it is worth noting that *Publisher's Weekly* determined, as of 2001, that *Green Eggs and Ham* was the fourth bestselling English language children's book of all time, up to that year.[115] The next reference "I Tawt I Saw A Puddy Tat" is both the classic line associated with iconic Warner Brothers/Looney Tunes character Tweety Bird and was also a 1950 song ("I Taut I Taw a Puddy Tat" by Tweety Pie featuring Sylvester The Cat).[116] After a few more lines, another pop culture reference hits the listener, as Meth pays homage to pioneering 1970s urban cartoon figure, Fat Albert, with the line "Hey, hey, hey like Fat Albert" ("hey, hey, hey" being the catchphrase used by Fat Albert during his eponymous show and, most famously, in the cartoon's theme song).[117]

The references don't stop there. In the second verse, Method Man melodically raps "Wrote a song about it, want to hear it, here it go," referencing a popular skit on 90s variety show *In Living Color*, where David Alan Grier played a blues artist named Calhoun Tubbs who introduced all his songs with the catchphrase "I wrote a song about it. Want to hear it? Here it go!"'[118]

Shifting from the world of television back to music, Meth's next reference ("I be the Super

Sporm") comes from 1978 song "Super Sporm" by Captain Sky.[119] Unexpectedly, Method Man even references Dick Van Dyke, by rapping "chim chim cheree" (a reference to the 1978 song "Chim Chim Cheree" by Dick Van Dyke, Julie Andrews, Karen Dotrice and Matthew Garber, off of the *Mary Poppins* soundtrack).[120] The last pop culture shoutout in the song ("How many licks does it take/to get to the Tootsie Roll center of a break") is a reference to the revered 1970 Tootsie Roll ad campaign, where viewers were challenged to guess how many licks it would take to get to the chewable interior of a Tootsie Roll lollipop.[121]

Method Man was acutely aware that incorporating pop culture references in his lyrics would make his music accessible to a wide range of people. "My method of rhyming, I don't know, I just say everything that everybody like to hear. I take it back. Way, way back to the days when you [were] waking up early in the morning [to see] Saturday morning cartoons. People recognize [the references], they hear stuff like that, and when you say stuff people are familiar with, it becomes fun for *them* to say," Meth reflected, when asked about his pop culture laden style in a 1994 interview.[122]

Method Man's ability to recontextualize cultural references also can be seen in his crafting of two of the catchiest choruses on *ETWT*. His hook on "Method Man" cleverly interpolated the hook from 1985 Hall & Oates pop smash

"Method of Modern Love." Method Man also crafted the winning hook for *ETWT*'s most successful single, "C.R.E.A.M." (Cash Rules Everything Around Me). Part of the "C.R.E.A.M." hook borrows from the chorus of veteran hip-hop artist Jimmy Spicer's "Money (Dollar Dollar Bill, Y'all)," released in 1983, ten years before *ETWT*. The chorus of "Money" would be very familiar to long-time hip-hop listeners, particularly in the tri-state area, and is another example of Wu-Tang keeping foundational hip-hop traditions alive (both sonically and through incorporation by reference). It is also indicative of Method Man's uncanny knack for choosing references that resonate with listeners.

Of course, there are many Clan members who made memorable contributions to the vocal side of *ETWT*, particularly in the area of crafting memorable hooks. For example, Rza handled the classic "Wu-Tang Clan Ain't Nuthin' To F' Wit" and "Bring Da Ruckus" hooks himself. ODB's wild stylings on the hook for "Shame On A Nigga" are also forever embedded in the memory of many hip-hop fans.

Furthermore, Meth isn't the only Clan member who had the privilege of having a solo track on *ETWT*. That is a privilege he shares with the leading lyricist in the Clan: the Gza. It could be argued that spotlighting "Clan In Da Front" as one of only two solo cuts on *ETWT* demonstrated the Clan's reverence for Gza. This decision also solidified the impression that the group viewed Gza as the group's premier lyricist.[123] The hook for "Clan In Da Front" is an evocative example of Gza's mastery as a writer, as the hook is carefully crafted so almost every line has the same number of syllables, to maximize its percussive effect and catchiness.

Even solo tracks on *ETWT* strategically keep the whole group front and center, as proven by Rza's decision to list the name of every member of the Clan and their assorted affiliates at the beginning of "Clan In Da Front." Perhaps as an indication of his importance to the group, Ghostface Killah is named twice (both before everyone else and again when the individual group members are named).[124] This decision to name the members of the Clan prior to the start of a solo track also occurred in the intro to "Method Man," where it was Gza who ran down the roll call of Wu members.

It is an interesting stylistic choice, as if Rza decided he wanted to let the world know how many individuals make up the Clan before allowing any individual emcee to take the spotlight. Nonetheless, Rza's decision to give Method Man and Gza the only solo tracks on the album seemed calculated to do just that: allow both emcees to shine. As if to repay the favor, Gza dedicated the end of the final verse on his solo song to praising Rza, by saying "and my DJ, the catcher, he's my man/in a way, he's the one who devised the plan."

Part of Rza's plan involved incorporating martial arts into *ETWT*. "Clan In Da Front" continues the album's martial arts theme when Gza references the 1982 film *The Shaolin Drunken Monk* in the first verse of "Clan In Da Front," by rapping the line "Here comes the drunk monk, with a quart of Ballantine."[125] This line is a clever blend of hip-hop tradition and martial arts film iconography: Ballantine was a favored drink in the golden era of hip-hop and the drunken monk character was a frequent motif in several martial arts films.[126]

The presence of martial arts film references throughout *ETWT* is part of the album's larger central theme of reminiscence—from invoking the films the Clan enjoyed as children to exploring the adversity they faced on the streets as young men. This theme of reminiscence continues on "Can It Be All So Simple,"[127] present in both the intro—where Rza enthusiastically describes his favorite years in the 80s—and the song's incorporation of a soul sample evocative of the records the Clan heard in their youth. With passionate performances from both Raekwon and Ghost, this song serves as the album's emotional centerpiece—a languid, almost dreamlike exploration of the Clan's troubled past.

After "Can It Be" ends, there is a skit of the Clan being interviewed on the radio, starting with Method Man breaking down all the members of the Clan and what their names signify. All the group members' names have been called out twice already by this point in the album (both here and in the "Clan In Da Front" intro). This running theme of identifying every Clan member continues on "Da Mystery of Chessboxin'," when Ol' Dirty Bastard runs down the names of the entire Clan (for the third time on the record) at the end of his verse.[128]

As mentioned earlier, a similar roll call would occur again on the album on the intro to "Method Man." This repetition of the names of all the members throughout the album appears to have been a deliberate move by Rza to assure that the listener became fully acquainted with each member of the Clan, a clever marketing move considering Rza's plan to launch solo careers for each member, following the release of *ETWT*.[129]

Method Man isn't the only Clan member who is a master of pop culture references. On his "Da Mystery of Chessboxin" verse, Ghostface blends pop culture with the NGE doctrine that the black man is god by flipping the old cliché "speaking of the devil" on its head, by declaring "Speaking of the devil, psyche, it's the god, get your shit right."[130] Inspectah Deck brags on his "Protect Ya Neck" verse that you can catch him "swingin' through your town like your neighborhood Spider-Man."[131]

Not to be outdone, Rza packs in the pop culture references on his "Wu-Tang Clan Ain't Nothing to F' Wit" verse, referencing both Marvel Comics' Dr. Doom and Tarzan within a few lines of one another. This verse is also an opportunity for Rza to show off his macabre sense of humor, in conjunction with his pop sensibility, as he turns a game show reference horrific, by boasting that he's "causing more family feuds than Richard Dawson/and the survey says...you're dead!"

In the same verse, Rza continues the motif of paralleling the Clan's verbal style with martial arts combat styles by boasting that his style is a "fatal flying guillotine [that] chops off your fucking head," likely a reference to the 1977 film *Fatal Flying Guillotine.*[132] To further demonstrate Rza's interest in reaching a broad audience across the country, instead of limiting the Clan's appeal to New York City, Rza ends the song by shouting out cities and states throughout America, from California to Texas (even squeezing in HBCU Morgan State University).

Other tracks on the record focus more on NGE teachings mixed with gritty street tales, most notably on "C.R.E.A.M." Cinematically, "C.R.E.A.M." opens with Raekwon re-enacting selling drugs on the corner (repeatedly saying "two for five's," i.e. advertising the sale price of two vials of crack for five dollars).[133] Raekwon's verse vividly describes his life as a dope dealer on the streets of New York. Inspectah Deck balances this portrayal out by showing the consequences of a criminal lifestyle (incarceration) while also referencing NGE coded language with the line "Ready to give up, so I seek the Old Earth" ("old earth" is NGE terminology for "mother").[134] "C.R.E.A.M." would go on to become the most successful single from the album, eventually selling over half a million copies.

After the heavy emotional content of "C.R.E.A.M.," Rza lightens the proceedings a bit with some gallows humor. In what has come to be known as the "Torture" skit, Method Man and Raekwon exchange hilarious boasts about the most over-the-top ways they can hypothetically harm one another (with Method Man apparently winning by threatening to sew Raekwon's anus shut and continually feed him, a threat that may have inspired the gluttony scene in the serial killer film *Seven*). This humorous skit serves as the perfect lead-in to one of the more fun selections on the album, "Method Man," which is then followed by "Protect Ya Neck" and "Tearz." Rza seems to have deliberately positioned all of the songs released before *ETWT* at the end of the tracklisting, perhaps being more interested in exposing listeners to Wu songs they had never heard.

The last song on the album is "Wu-Tang: 7th Chamber Part II," which begins with the hook from "Clan In Da Front" (seeming to actually sample Gza's voice) and features a different beat (and spoken intro) from the other version of "7th Chamber."[135] Aside from these changes, "Wu-Tang: 7th Chamber Part II" is otherwise essentially identical to Part 1. The album closes with a martial arts film sample,

"Never teach the secret of the Wu-Tang," which gives the listener the feeling that he or she has been inducted into a secret club, just by hearing the album.

The feeling of secrecy surrounding the Clan even permeated *ETWT*'s cover artwork, which featured several members of the Clan clad in masks. Daniel Hastings is the photographer credited with shooting the album cover, although contemporary recollection regarding who came up with the idea of shooting the group wearing masks is a bit hazy, now that twenty years has passed since the cover shoot occurred. Art coordinator Liz Fierro, who oversaw the photo shoot for *ETWT*'s classic cover, recalled that several group members were absent on the day of the shoot and said it was decided that the Clan should be shot wearing masks (presumptively because if they appeared unmasked, it would be clear which members were not present, once the album came out).

"The idea for [the album cover] was a collaborative effort," Fierro recalled. "We had gotten a bunch of props—masks and hats and hoodies…and there were some members who didn't show up, so we decided to put masks on the members who were there. We also Vaselined the lens on Daniel Hastings' camera so it would give that effect of being really eerie and so nothing would be sharp. They wanted [to wear] the masks, as well, though. I don't think we would have brought stockings on our own."[136]

Jackie Murphy, art director for the *ETWT* cover shoot, had a slightly different recollection of how the issue of the missing members was addressed (as even wearing masks wouldn't prevent a clever Wu fan from merely counting the people on the cover and realizing some Clan members were missing). "Daniel and I knew we had some missing members and we had these masks already as props," Murphy recollected. "So because we had some absent members that day we put two of the managers in the shot."[137] Quite a few members must have been absent from the shoot, however, as only seven figures can be seen on the album cover.

According to the cover photographer, Daniel Hastings, the idea to have the Clan wear masks on their album cover was inspired by a real life incident, when the Clan (clad in masks) rushed the stage to eject another performing act at the (ironically titled) Jack The Rapper convention in Atlanta. The group then began to perform "Wu-Tang Clan Ain't Nuthin' To F' Wit," to the delight of the crowd.

Hastings would recall the frenetic energy of that moment much later when the time came to decide how to salvage the *ETWT* photo shoot. "We're expecting [the whole group], but what we get is only like [six] people. It was RZA, ODB, Ghostface, Inspectah Deck, the GZA [and Raekwon]. U-God, Method Man, and Masta Killa did not come for some particular reason," Hastings recalled.[138] "And I was like, 'Yo, what if we do what you guys did [at Jack the Rapper]?' If I didn't go to Atlanta [and see the Wu-Tang perform], I don't think the stocking masks [on the cover] would have happened. They were like, 'You're not showing our faces?' I'm like, 'Yeah, man, you guys are the Wu-Tang Clan. You're selling the Wu-Tang Clan. Let's do this. Let's get some hoodies, put the logo on there.' They had stickers so they put them on their hoodies…and RZA liked the idea. So we went in and did it."[139]

The resulting iconic cover undoubtedly added to the air of mystery surrounding the Clan. If the Clan could be considered a closely held secret amongst a select few fans in the group's early days, this would not be the case for long, as their debut album would go on to sell well over a million copies.

Chapter 4: Culture

The sound of *Enter the Wu-Tang* is drawn from so many musical genres and cinematic sources that the album was virtually guaranteed to appeal across cultures, globally. Studying the sample sources that appear on it, track by track, should clearly demonstrate why *ETWT* was accessible to such a diverse range of people.

The album opens with the explosive track "Bring Da Ruckus," which features Rza screaming "bring the motherfucking ruckus!" repeatedly as the song's hook. To add to the chaos, the track features finger snaps and piano "stabs," each battling for the attention of the listener.[140] However, the most prominent feature of "Bring Da Ruckus" is the drums, recorded with an echo effect that makes them sound like they were played underwater.

Those iconic, oft-sampled drums—derived from "Synthetic Substitution" by Melvin Bliss—are the first musical sound you hear on *ETWT*, immediately after the series of kung fu vocal samples that open the album. It is a fitting opening for two reasons. For one, the song from which the drums are borrowed, "Synthetic Substitution," decries unnatural forces taking over the country, while the entire ethos of Wu-Tang represents opposition to the unnatural corporate influence then (and now) overtaking hip-hop culture.[141] For two, the choice of this well-loved breakbeat subtly informs the listener that the archetypal breakbeat culture that serves as the foundation of hip-hop will be central to *ETWT*. This drum pattern is sampled twice more on the album, on "Clan In Da Front" and "Method Man" respectively, for a total of three uses throughout the record.[142]

With all the energy unleashed by the opening track, one might expect that the album's momentum can only go down from there. To the contrary, the album's second track, "Shame On A Nigga," opens with possibly the most energetic Method Man performance captured on wax. Rza weaves a sample from Syl Johnson's "Different Strokes" throughout "Shame," most prominently underneath the song's hyperkinetic chorus, provided by Ol' Dirty Bastard.[143] "Different Strokes" is a heavily sampled composition, so Rza's decision to use only a snippet of it is clever, as just enough of it is sampled to spark the sense memory of any longtime hip-hop fan, without the completed beat sounding too much like other tracks that have used the same sample. Finally, the piano sample in "Shame" is an inspired usage of the opening of Thelonious Monk's 1955 cover of Duke Ellington composition "Black and Tan Fantasy" (1927). By intertwining these two samples and combining them with dynamic vocal performances from Method Man and Ol' Dirty Bastard, Rza incredibly brings together seven decades of black music and three separate genres, on one song!

The intro (and a breakdown at 2:27) of New Birth's "Honey Bee" is the foundation of "Clan In Da Front." It is unclear whether Rza already intended to refer to Wu-Tang Clan as "killer bees" before sampling this track or if Rza was inspired by the sound of bees in the intro of "Honey Bee" to scream "Wu-Tang Killa Bees on a swarm" on the intro of "Clan In Da Front." In either case, this killer bee motif would last throughout much of the Wu's career, even inspiring the storyline of the video for their sophomore album's lead single, "Triumph," where Wu-Tang Clan is portrayed as a swarm of killer bees that transforms back into human form to attack New York City.[144]

In perhaps another example of Rza paying homage to the hip-hop classics that came before the Clan, the drums A Tribe Called Quest sampled for their classic single "Can I Kick It?" (from their debut record, *Peoples Instinctive Travels In The Paths of Rhythm*) are also used in the next track on *ETWT*, "Wu-Tang: 7th Chamber." Both songs sample these drums from Lonnie Liston Smith's "Spinning Wheel."

Crossing space and time in a way that only sampling can facilitate, the spoken intro to Gladys Knight and The Pips "The Way We Were" is recontextualized as a spoken intro for "Can It Be All So Simple," with Raekwon going back and forth with Gladys Knight's sampled dialogue. The first nine words sung in the sampled Knight song ("Can it be that it was all so simple") are pitch shifted down and used as the hook for the Clan's track, the title of which is a shortened version of this opening line.[145] The reminiscing theme of the original is carried through on the Clan's version, as Ghost and Raekwon reflect on life growing up in their respective housing projects on Staten Island (whereas Ms. Knight sang of a past love).

"The Way We Were" was originally sung by Barbara Streisand, 20 years prior to the release of *ETWT*.[146] This is a further example of the type of cross-cultural reach that is possible via the transformative nature of sampling: connecting worlds (two housing projects on Staten Island and the Brooklyn neighborhood where Streisand grew up) culturally light years apart, yet physically only mere miles away. In this instance, sampling can be seen as a metaphor for the multicultural experience of life in New York City itself, the musical version of a melting pot.

Although Rza used heavily sampled breakbeats throughout the album, he also beat several producers to the punch with his usage of the second sample in "Can It All Be So Simple": Labi Siffre's "I Got The." The piano in Siffre's composition is slowed down dramatically—to an almost hypnotic pace—for the melody on "Can It Be All So Simple." Post-Wu icons Jay-Z ("Streets Is Watching") and Eminem (for his breakout debut single "My Name Is") would both later sample this same song, but neither producer of these subsequent songs (Ski and Dr. Dre, respectively) would sample "I Got The" in as subtle a fashion as Rza. In another tribute to how sampling brings together disparate worlds, Siffre was multiculturalism incarnate: openly gay and born in Britain, he was the son of a Barbadian/Belgian mother and a Nigerian father.[147] Thus, through the samples it incorporates, "Can It Be All So Simple" encompasses experiences from West Africa, Western Europe, The Caribbean, Black America, Jewish America, straight America and gay Europe, by sonic osmosis, all blended together into a potent musical medley.

Whether Rza intended to expand the Wu's cultural reach through sample selections from artists like Siffre may be debatable, but what is not arguable is Rza's commitment to incorporate hip-hop's foundation—breakbeats—into Wu's music. A fine example of this phenomenon is the incorporation of the drums from respected breakbeat "Hihache" by The Lafayette Afro Rock Band into "Wu-Tang Clan Ain't Nothing To F' Wit."[148] Yet it was Method Man, not Rza, who suggested the use of that particular drum sample and, as a result, Meth received co-production credit on the song.[149] "Hihache" contained an already well-loved drum breakdown, previously sampled on Biz Markie's "Nobody Beats The Biz."[150] Method Man's suggestion to Rza to sample this foundational breakbeat demonstrates the Clan's commitment to keeping hip-hop's sonic traditions alive.[151]

Suggesting that Rza use an evocative classic breakbeat was only part of Method Man's contribution to the accessibility of *ETWT*. As mentioned in the prior chapter, Method Man ingeniously chose to interpolate the "m-e-t-h-o-d" on the chorus of Hall and Oates' "Method of Modern Love" (1984) to etch his name into the minds of generations of music lovers.[152] "Method of Modern Love" rose as high as number five on the *Billboard* Hot 100 in February 1985; incorporating part of its chorus to spell Method Man's name is indicative of the pop alchemy exercised by the Wu (and hip-hop as a whole): the recontextualizing of beloved songs from other genres.

The blending and recontextualizing of hit songs from other eras on "Method Man" is further exemplified by Rza's decision to sample the bassline from the opening bars of 1974 #1 folk smash "Sundown" by Canadian folk singer, Gordon Lightfoot. This sample selection by Rza adds one more genre (folk) and another nationality (Canadian) to the melting pot vibe embodied throughout *ETWT*. To add yet another genre to the sonic mix comprising "Method Man," Rza also sampled the drums from breakbeat classic "Sport" by Lightnin' Rod (off of his 1973 *Hustlers Convention* album, a sampling staple in hip-hop and often cited as one of the first rap records, due to the rhymed couplets "rapped" by Lightnin' Rod on the record). Besides being a cornerstone of rap music, the

Hustlers Convention LP also features excellent backing music by funk legends Kool and the Gang, so Rza was able to tap yet another genre (funk) with this sample selection, to widen the cultural reach of *ETWT* even further.

The opening of Wendy Rene's soul gem "After Laughter Comes Tears" provides both the hook and the main musical melody of "Tearz," a re-titled version of the first song recorded under the Wu-Tang banner (originally titled "After The Laughter Comes Tears"). Eradicating geographic barriers, the blending of the hardcore New York hip-hop of the Clan and Rene's Southern soul was a powerful combination.[153]

Wendy Rene is not the only female vocalist whose work was recontextualized by the Clan. The most prominent "sample" in "Protect Ya Neck" is Method Man's savvy decision to interpolate the best known part of the hook ("Fame, I'm gonna live forever") from Irene Cara's "Fame" into his verse ("Like 'Fame', my style will live forever"), another cross-cultural moment of brilliance on *ETWT*.[154] Also known as the theme for the TV adaptation of *Fame* (a cover version), the Cara original reached #4 on the pop charts in 1980, won an Oscar for Best Original Song the same year, and no doubt would still be embedded in the subconscious of many rap fans when *ETWT* was released in 1993.[155] It's yet another example of how Method Man was particularly adept at weaving pop culture references into his music, expanding the accessibility of the Wu's music dramatically.

It is apropos that the musical film *Fame* would inspire Method Man to interpolate a line from its theme, since Rza aspired to create music that was the audio version of film (essentially musicals without a visual component). "There were no DVDs in those days, so my idea was that people would get these one-hour audio movies. I did the whole thing with a movie concept," Rza said, when describing his production style in an interview.[156]

In a separate interview, Rza expanded on this idea of his records serving as the audio equivalent of films. "My fantasy was to make a one-hour movie that people were just going to *listen* to. They would hear my movie and see it in their minds. I'd read comic books like that, with sonic effects and kung fu voices in my head. That makes it more exciting, so I try to create music in the same way."[157]

It's no secret that martial arts films heavily influenced *ETWT*. The album's subtitle (*36 Chambers*) is inspired by the film *The 36th Chamber of Shaolin* (also known in America as *Master Killer*, the source of another Clan member's name).[158] That film was directed by Lau Kar-Leong, who started as an actor in martial arts films, then evolved into a choreographer, and finally became a director.[159] Lau's action-oriented background likely enabled him to lend authenticity to the fight scenes in *The 36th Chamber.* Additionally, Lau specifically sought to hire actors with martial arts training, to insure the quality of that film's action sequences.[160] The authentic nature of the action in *The 36th Chamber* probably helped endear that film to members of the Wu and was likely the type of authenticity, in the realm of hip-hop, that the Wu strived to embody with their debut record.

Shaolin & Wutang was another film that had a major influence on the group. That film is not only the source of the group's name, it is also the origin of many of the vocal samples on the album. Rza's decision to utilize lines from *Shaolin & Wutang* to open and close the album arguably indicates how much that film influenced the Clan.[161] The film is sampled in the body of the album as well. The Wu-Tang master in *Shaolin & Wu-Tang* delivers the line "The game of chess is like a swordfight. You must think first before you move"—Rza uses this line to open "Da Mystery of Chessboxin'."

Speaking on why he chose to utilize that particular vocal sample, Rza described its value as a "jewel."[162] "It had great resonance with what we were doing. It was a great sentence. It makes sense in everyday life. A game of chess *is* like a swordfight. You must think first before you move. In chess, people don't think first before they move, nor in fighting do they think before they move. It's a great jewel, a great aphorism for all of us to hear. And it worked perfect[ly] as an intro to the song," Rza said.[163]

That was not the only jewel that Rza found in films he enjoyed. He explained in a 2005 interview how he gradually found deeper meaning in martial arts films as he continued to watch them. "I started listening to what they were saying about brotherhood, loyalty, [and] patriotism, some of the words Buddha had taught them," Rza said. "What I did was I took these elements from all over. The word 'wu' means 'martial arts'. I like to use acronyms for things. The W is for 'wisdom', the U is for 'universal': the wisdom of the universe."[164]

"Those films represented what we were standing for, in the position of the hip-hop we were bringing in. They said what I wanted to say. And they said it using those words and those old styles," Rza reflected, in a recent interview. "I could have said it myself, [imitating the sample] 'If what you say is true, the Wu-Tang could be dangerous', but there is something unique about those old films and those old recordings, the [sound] quality [that I wanted to preserve]. As a DJ, I wanted to add that to our music. You couldn't take it from one movie, you had to cut from here and cut from there, but that's what DJ's do, you cut from different records to make a groove."[165]

In a separate interview in 2013, Rza expounded on the connection between Wu-Tang Clan and *Shaolin & Wu-Tang*. "We named our neighborhood, our Staten Island borough, Shaolin," Rza explained. "We were the ones coming out of Shaolin. In the movie *Shaolin & Wu-Tang*, one of the movies that inspired us, the Wu-Tang founder...was a student of Shaolin. Then, he leaves Shaolin and goes to Wu-Dang Mountain. He meditates [by] himself and finds out that martial arts can be done internally... coming from Shaolin, going to Wu-Tang, then spreading from there, is how I felt we were...we came from this location [Staten Island/Shaolin] and we went around the world and spread our hip-hop culture, then we returned back to Shaolin, as our foundation."[166]

Several members of the Wu-Tang Clan derived their stage names from kung fu films. *The Fearless Young Boxer* (1979) was a film that was released on video in the United States as *Method Man* and is possibly the source of Method Man's name.[167] As mentioned earlier, Ghostface Killer derived his name from the villain in the film *Mystery of Chessboxing*. It seems likely that Ol' Dirty Bastard derived his stage name from the 1980 film *An Old Kung Fu Master*, which had the alternate title *Ol' Dirty and the Bastard*.[168] As previously mentioned, Masta Killa derived his name from a central character in *The 36th Chamber of Shaolin* (released in the US under the title *The Master Killer*).

Martial arts film references even make their way into the lyrics of the album, such as on "Shame on a Nigga," when Ol' Dirty Bastard excitedly proclaims "Here comes the Tiger verse Crane," possibly referencing the 1976 film *Tiger and Crane Fist.*[169] There are several non-martial arts film references throughout the album as well, such as when Ol' Dirty references 1979 film *The Warriors*, also on "Shame," by singing "Warriors come out to play!" (an iconic line from that film).

While the New York City gang warfare present in *The Warriors* fits the rugged theme of the album, Gza's reference to 1947 Christmas film *A Miracle On 34th Street* in the first verse of "Clan In Da Front" is more surprising, if only due to the contrast between that film's light-hearted tone and the more combative sound of *ETWT* (as such, this is the perfect demonstration of the pop culture melting pot effect present throughout the album). Notably, this reference still centers on a film based in New York City, specifically 34th Street. Gza's *Miracle on 34th Street* reference is immediately followed by a line name-checking the Herald Square subway stop, which is located where 34th Street and Broadway intersect.

The film theme continues throughout Gza's opening verse on "Clan In Da Front," where he weaved the film titles *Indiana Jones*, *The Mack*, *Dolemite*, *Claudine*, *Cooley High*, and *Full Metal Jacket* into a series of metaphoric references.[170] The middle four films in this sequence of references are all black film classics from the 70s, the era that appears most influential on *ETWT*. Many of the martial arts films referenced or sampled in the album were produced in (or near) that decade as well.

The Wu's love of film even extends to the skits on *ETWT*, including one skit where Raekwon admonishes Method Man for losing a VHS tape of classic John Woo film, *The Killer*. True to the Wu's rock star reputation, Meth responds that associates came by with beer and marijuana and the tape "came up missing." The skit was based on a real incident. Raekwon admitted in an interview that, almost twenty years after the album was recorded, he still has not gotten his *Killer* tape back from Meth.[171]

Nineteen years after *ETWT* was released, Rza brought the connection between Wu and film full circle. When Rza made his directorial debut with *The Man With Iron Fists*, he assured that the first sound that audiences heard when they viewed the film was the voice of Ol' Dirty Bastard. "We used to watch all those movies together," Rza explained when discussing his decision to open the film with Ol Dirty's rapping. "He didn't get to see the dream come to life, so I decided the first thing [the audience was] going to hear is [Dirty]."[172]

Chapter 5: Power

The Clan built one of the most powerful global brands in hip-hop, based on an international vision that they could make music that would rock the world. In a 2005 interview with *The Daily Show*, Rza explained how he saw commonality across cultures. "There's a common thread, whether you come from Asian culture, European culture, American culture—there are so many threads we overlook and I strive to bring those threads together," Rza explained.[173] He then got a laugh from the *Daily Show* crowd by explaining how this cultural spin on the unified field theory led the Clan to draw from a diverse range of influences in their work. "One minute, we're quoting from The Bible and the next moment, we're quoting from Marvel Comics."

Utilizing the power of hip-hop to combine cultures, Rza was able to make *ETWT* appeal to people around the world. To help bring his vision to fruition, a diverse group worked on the album with him. As previously mentioned, the album's cover was shot by Daniel Hastings, an eighteen-year-old Panamanian-American.[174] A white Jewish man named Ethan Ryman is credited with engineering most of the album, with the exception of "Da Mystery of Chessboxin'," the engineering of which is credited to Carlos Bess, who is Latino.[175]

In an interesting case of the memory of participants differing from what appears in the official album credits, Firehouse studio owner Yoram Vazan recalled that Bess also engineered the session for "Protect Ya Neck" and "After The Laughter" (which eventually became "Tearz"), although he received no credit for this in the *ETWT* liner notes.[176] "They did 'Protect Ya Neck' and I forgot what was on the B-side ['After the Laughter Comes Tears']," Vazan recalled. "I let one of my new engineers, Carlos Bess, do it."[177]

Rza is credited with mixing the entire album, but he and Ryman (or Bess, depending on the session) were hardly the only people in the studio. Ryman recalls the *ETWT* recording sessions being a serious undertaking, for which the entire Clan showed up. "When we started recording *Enter The Wu-Tang*, the whole group was usually there for every session. Sometimes it felt like their whole neighborhood was in the studio," Ryman recalled. "Every now and then, RZA and I would have to clear the room so we could get to the equipment. I remember feeling there was a very forceful energy with them. They were not playing around."[178]

Ryman recalls a particularly humorous interaction with the late Ol' Dirty Bastard during the recording process for *ETWT*. "ODB was, I think, the first vocal we did—'Shame On A Nigga,' maybe. He's in the vocal room and I adjust the large boom mic over his head, give him his headphones and show him how to adjust the volume and where to stand. Then I go back to the control room to get the levels and make sure he's comfortable with everything. So I'm looking at him through the glass and he's kind of fidgeting and playing with his hands and looking nervous and I thought maybe he wasn't used to being in the studio and was used to having a mic in his hand, like on stage. So I push the talk-back button and say to him something like, 'Yo, if you're used to holding something, I can get you something to hold,' meaning I would get him a handheld mic, if it would make him more comfortable. He starts laughing and shaking his head because he thinks I was telling him that if he was scared he could hold my dick! We got along well after that."[179]

Yoram Vazan, the owner of Firehouse (where the album was recorded) and, like Ryman, also coincidentally a white Jewish man, has a humorous anecdote about the Clan as well. "I remember they used to pay me with quarters!" Vazan recalled in animated fashion. Vazan seemed to take this unusual payment method in stride, in addition to reminiscing on occasions when he wasn't paid at all. "It was so funny. At that point I knew them for a few years; I always told them, 'Don't worry about it, you'll come back.'"[180]

The mastering engineer for the record, Chris Gehringer, was white as well. Although he went on to work with commercial powerhouses such as Lady Gaga and Rihanna, Gehringer's career was jumpstarted by his early work with the Clan.[181] Gehringer recalls working closely with Rza to help him reach his sonic goal with *ETWT*, utilizing the somewhat limited technology available to them both at the time. "We literally took a VHS machine and copied [the kung fu samples] RZA wanted off the VHS machine and onto a DAT player and edited those pieces in," Gehringer recalled. "This was back in the days of pre-audio and computer workstations, so we were using digital editors that couldn't cross-fade more than half a second and they had a lot of those skits that they had to slide in. It was probably more work putting that part of the album together than anything else."[182]

Like Ryman, Gehringer noticed the Clan's dedication to the recording process. That dedication extended all the way to the final stage when Gehringer became involved: mastering (where sonic levels of all the songs on the record are calibrated so the album has a consistent sound quality throughout). "Most of the group were in [the room] for the album mastering," Gehringer recalled.[183] It is slightly unusual for an entire rap group to show up for mastering, so this demonstrates how much commitment the Wu had to making sure *ETWT* was a great album. That commitment is what enabled *ETWT* to resonate around the world.

That global resonance is unsurprising, considering Rza's international outlook, which originated from his passion for films produced thousands of miles from where he lived. Interestingly, as Rza more closely studied the history of martial arts films, he learned that overdubbed versions of the films that had profoundly affected him contained completely inaccurate translations. "I came to find out that the words that were said [in the English overdubbed versions of his favorite martial arts films] aren't what the translation really said....it's a good thing and a bad thing," Rza noted, before providing a positive spin on this state of affairs. "The good thing is, there's no way for them to say we infringed on their movie…some of the samples I used and the movies I got them from weren't even really popular. To me, [those movies] fit in my world better than [they] fit in…the world [in which] they were created."[184]

Over time, Rza also discovered that sometimes how he perceived these films was not how their creators intended their audience to perceive them. "The movie *36 Chambers* had a profound spiritual effect on me, but if you listen to the [DVD] commentary, the director and the actors thought they were being funny on some things," Rza recalled, solemnly. "But it wasn't funny to me."[185]

Similar to how Chinese film profoundly affected Rza, the English language work of the Clan would later become the first introduction to both English and hip-hop for others around the world. A Norwegian kicker for the Detroit Lions, Havard Rugland, recently revealed that he learned English by listening to Wu-Tang Clan.[186] Thousands of miles east of Norway, *ETWT* inspired one of the youngest mainstream rappers in South Korea, G-Dragon, to pursue a music career, at the tender age of five. "I started rapping because of that album," G-Dragon said. "I'm not fluent in English now, but back then I didn't know anything. I would write down the lyrics to 'C.R.E.A.M.' in Korean, not translating it, but phonetically writing out each word."[187] G-Dragon's admission that he could not even speak English at the time that he first heard the album, yet was still captivated enough to attempt to transcribe some of the lyrics, proves the international appeal of *ETWT*.

The Clan also made decisions regarding their visual presentation that would later have an international effect as well. The bling-bling imagery of hip-hop videos in the late nineties promoted an image worldwide of black wealth that was a far cry from the daily financial reality for most African-Americans. One video director is largely responsible for that (skewed) representation and his success (and subsequent impact on global culture) is largely owed to the Clan's early decision to work with that particular director: Hype Williams.

Admittedly, Williams had shot videos for several years before he shot "Can It Be All So Simple" for Wu-Tang Clan, but this 1994 video was his first to get heavy airplay. Soon thereafter, he shot the video for rising Bad Boy star Craig Mack's "Flava In Ya Ear (remix)" and went on to become arguably the most successful music video director of all time (with a string of seven figure budget videos to his credit). Williams would later pay back the favor to Wu by casting Method Man in a key role in his directorial debut, *Belly*, the breakout moment in Method Man's acting career, which is in its sixteenth year at the time of this writing.[188]

The video for "Can It Be All So Simple" is the best-directed video from *ETWT* and most likely had the largest budget (or so it seems, judging by the stark difference in visual quality between this video and the videos for "Method Man," "Protect Ya Neck" and "Da Mystery of Chessboxin").[189] The hypnotic dissolves and slow motion shots throughout the video fit the somber mood and slower tempo of "Can It All Be So Simple" perfectly. Many of the shots parallel (but rarely literally follow) the lyrics in inventive fashion, such as the inclusion of a cameo from Crip-affiliated West Coast rapper MC Eiht at the 2:16 mark of the video, concurrent with the section of the song where Raekwon shouts out "niggas who do drive-bys."[190] The inclusion of MC Eiht in this video was also groundbreaking at a time when some East Coast rap artists expressed disdain for the West Coast, likely in reaction to the latter's commercial dominance over the mainstream at that time.[191]

Shots of children throughout the video also reflected a break from traditional rap video imagery at the time, particularly a closing shot with Method Man posing with his infant for the camera. Childhood, of course, is central to the reminiscing theme of the song. That reminiscing theme is best illustrated in the brilliantly choreographed opening scene, where Rza's vocal intro discussing the best years in the 80s is acted out with expert precision.

"Can It Be All So Simple" also inadvertently demonstrated the impact of Wu on the world of fashion. Over time, the rare Ralph Lauren Snow Beach pullover worn by Raekwon in the video has become an object of obsession for many collectors of Polo gear. Almost twenty years after the video debuted, the online version of *Complex Magazine* even went as far as to rank Raekwon's decision to wear the Snow Beach pullover #2 in its list of the top 50 fashion moments in rap video history.[192]

Williams wasn't the only director to visually interpret the songs from *ETWT*. Gerald Barclay directed "Method Man," the second video ever shot by the Clan, as well as the video for "Da Mystery of Chessboxin'."[193] Both videos were low budget, but powerfully captured the live performance energy of the Clan. Many of the stylistic motifs of the group's artwork for the album were reflected in the video for "Da Mystery of Chessboxin'," including the decision to have several members (and extras) masked throughout the video (including Method Man and Ghostface), similar to how the group's faces were obscured by masks on the now classic *ETWT* cover. Some members also wore Wu-Tang promotional stickers adhered to their hooded sweatshirts, another visual allusion to the album cover.

As Raekwon raps in the "Chessboxin" video, Ghostface stands to his left, wearing a keffiyeh wrapped around his face in a style similar to Palestinian militants, and the phrase "P.L.O. Style" is spray-painted on the wall behind them, adding yet another cultural layer to the global appeal of the Wu-Tang Clan. Ol' Dirty Bastard's performance in the video is the standout, due to both his energy and the unique way his scene is shot. Barclay shoots ODB from above and at a diagonal angle (whereas the video's other performances are shot in a more traditional fashion).

The chess motif appears throughout the video, with Barclay occasionally cutting away from the performers to shots of unspoken group leaders Rza and Gza pensively analyzing a chess board while Wu members (and extras) portray life-sized chess pieces, wearing either white or black hooded sweatshirts, to represent black or white chess pieces. It's a brilliant and subtle statement demonstrating the influence that Rza and Gza had over the direction of the group, visually implying that they are controlling the Clan members' every move.

In keeping with the *ETWT* theme contrasting swordplay with Wu's lyrics, Masta

Killa swings swords in the video, while referencing swordplay in his verse. The combination of chess and martial arts swordsmanship connect Wu-Tang to eastern traditions that span back millennia—chess from the Middle East and martial arts from the Far East.

Years after his early video work with the Wu, Gerald Barclay would go on to direct the *Wu: The Story of the Wu-Tang Clan* documentary on the group. In a DVD extra feature shot for this documentary, Barclay recounted how he was specifically instructed to never capture Ghost's face on camera in either of the videos he directed (perhaps to maintain the early motif of Ghost being a masked assassin—literally a ghost-faced killer).[194]

Aside from the aforementioned videos financed by Loud, one should not discount the visual impact of the video the Wu financed themselves, when they were still independent artists. Despite what appears to be a minimal budget, the video for "Protect Ya Neck" perfectly captures the group's magnetic showmanship, with its searing imagery positioning the Clan almost like swordsmen in some post-apocalyptic dystopian future. Rza co-directed this raucous video featuring the Clan and roughly two-dozen of their compatriots as extras.

Gerald Barclay recalls Rza's split with Kurt Anthony,[195] the other co-director of "Protect

Ya Neck," as less than harmonious. "I forget the guy's name, but [him and Rza] did the video [for 'Protect Ya Neck'], and RZA called me and told me he was having problems with the guy," Barclay recalled. "So, [the Clan] took over the video, but I think [Anthony] only gave [Rza] the one set of reel that had the timecode on it…they didn't know the difference between an offline version and online version, and they just went with it. I think once he did that cut, they decided they were going to keep it as it was, which ended up becoming a classic."[196]

"Uncle" Ralph McDaniels was the first to play the video on television, on his iconic show, *Video Music Box.*[197] "Rza showed me [an early version of] 'Protect Ya Neck.' It wasn't finished yet. It had the timecode on it still. It didn't bother me though," McDaniels recalled. "It actually made it look raw, so I told Rza I [would] help him with it and that I would play the video."[198]

"Protect Ya Neck" also visually marks a transformation for both Rza and Gza, a re-branding of sorts, letting listeners know that their work with the Clan would bear little similarity to their pre-Clan solo work. When Rza's scene in the "Protect Ya Neck" video comes up, the text on the screen reads "Exit Prince Rakeem….enter The Rza," in order to announce his new persona to a hip-hop world then only familiar with him as Prince Rakeem. For fans accustomed to "Ooh I Love You, Rakeem," it must have been quite a startling transformation, yet welcome to the ears of any hardcore rap fan. When Gza appears onscreen in the video, the text on the screen reads "Jizah." In *The Wu-Tang Manual*, Rza describes J-I-Z-Z-A as the original spelling of Gza's name, a variation of the second half of Gza's divine name in NGE, Allah Justice.[199]

Music videos were not the only arena in which the Wu made a powerful impression. There is one area where Wu-Tang Clan reigns supreme in their genre, if not over their entire musical generation, and that is when the discussion turns to which group has the most iconic logo. While Public Enemy's beloved Chuck D-designed "man in the crosshairs" logo has emblazoned T-shirts for over twenty five years and the Hieroglyphics collective's Del-designed three eyed logo is the foundation of an indie merchandising empire that sells everything from $50 sweatshirts to $25 hats, the Wu logo reigns supreme.[200] In one interview, Ghostface Killah (who has no tattoos himself) expressed disbelief at the sheer number of times that he has encountered fans around the world who had the Wu-Tang logo tattooed onto their skin. "That Wu love—I recognized that shit when I went to Australia, New Zealand, that's the other side of the map [from where we grew up]—even Russia—they got tattoos on them…all the little motherfuckers with W's, they gonna die with that. I know motherfuckers already that died with Wu-Tang tattoos on them. What did we do to get [people to tattoo our logo on them]," Ghostface wondered aloud. "It's only a W, a fucking bird.

I'm like, goddamn, it's really that big? They going to the grave with that, with our emblem on their body. I don't even got one! No ink [on my skin], but they got it. They gonna be 80, 90 years old [with that on their skin]."[201]

Fans have even turned Wu's W-shaped logo into hand gestures to salute the group when they see them. In this spirit, Wu-Tang fans filling arenas are known to form their hands into the shape of W's at the sight of the Clan and tirelessly hold those W's high for hour-plus performances.

The designer of that iconic logo is longtime Wu-Tang DJ, Mathematics (who, along with True Master and 4th Disciple, is one of the few people on Earth—outside of Rza—to produce cuts on a Wu album). Remarkably, Mathematics recounted in one interview that he created the original version of the now world famous logo in a single day. "We tried a few different things, but when it came down to it—and Rza basically needed the logo the next day—that's the W that I did," Mathematics reflected.[202]

In a separate interview, he gave more details about the process of creating the logo. "Rza called me one day and was like 'I'm printing up this song tomorrow, yo. I need a logo and I need it by tomorrow'…at the time, I was staying in 40 Projects, in Queens. Sat down on the floor and came up with the original logo, with the W, the book, the sword and all that," Allah Mathematics explained. "I was working at the time as a carpenter. Rza was like 'I'm gonna pick it up from you tomorrow'. It was Rza, Ghost, Power and Divine. They came through my job, with the hoodies on, came rolling through and they all looked at it, [and were] like 'That's it.'"[203]

The Wu-Tang logo and the impact Rza had on re-introducing martial arts film culture into the mainstream would eventually lead to a mutually beneficial business arrangement between Rza and a film company that owned the rights to many of the films he sampled. "Remember the *Wu-Tang Collection* that came out later on? When the company that put those films out came to me, they said they wanted to use the Wu-Tang logo [on the cover of the DVD re-issue]. One thing I demanded—they paid money and shit [for the rights to use the logo]—but I wanted to be able to sample any movie [for which they owned rights,] at any time…I made that deal back in '97."[204]

Few modern music acts can claim to have a logo as recognizable and loved as the Wu-Tang W logo. It is so recognizable that, thousands of miles away from where the Wu was formed, film companies were willing to exchange both cash and the right to sample dialogue from their films for the right to use the Wu logo. That same logo would become the cornerstone of the Wu-Wear clothing empire, started by Wu business manager Oli "Power" Grant, which at its height would earn one million dollars in sales from one Staten Island-based store, in one year.[205] Finally, fans from around the world would tattoo the Wu logo on their flesh, a phenomenon that occurs with few acts of any genre. From videos to clothing to their logo, the visual impact of the Wu has spread internationally, all based on the power of a movement that started twenty years ago.

Chapter 6: Equality

Despite the large size of Wu-Tang Clan, they have never broken up, which is a frequent fate of many hip-hop groups. When one looks carefully at their history, it's not hard to see why the group has remained unified for over twenty years.

One likely reason why the Wu has been able to stay together is because the members of the Clan have known each other for most of their lives. Some even have blood ties. While being interviewed by fellow hip-hop artist Snoop Dogg, Rza revealed that Ol' Dirty Bastard's father and his grandmother were brother and sister.[206] Rza went on to explain that he and ODB knew each other since they were six, even taking baths with one another (an old tactic used by very poor households to conserve water, to save money).[207] In the same interview, Rza revealed that Gza was also his cousin, by marriage, and that Gza was the first person to introduce him to knowledge of self, i.e. the teachings of the Nation of Gods and Earths.[208] Rza, in turn, taught the lessons to Ghostface and Ol' Dirty Bastard.[209] Method Man and U-God have known one another since elementary school, while Gza has known Raekwon and Inspectah Deck since elementary school.[210] As aforementioned, Rza and Ghostface Killah grew up in Stapleton Houses together. Method Man and Rza met in the ninth grade. Rza and Raekwon have known each other since the second grade.[211] Some of the Wu bond is even intergenerational, as Raekwon revealed in one documentary that his mother and U-God's mother have been friends since high school.[212] In the same documentary, U-God recalled that he and Raekwon have known each other since they were four years old.[213]

There is also another reason that may explain the group's longevity. Rza's early decision to have group members split publishing revenue equally amongst the group likely eliminated the typical monetary disputes that lead to so many band breakups.[214] By assuring that the most successful and the least successful group members all shared publishing revenue generated by Wu songs equally, Rza assured that Wu could, for the most part, avoid envy or infighting over money. This magnanimous arrangement also gave each Wu member a vested interest in the success of his brothers.

Clan business manager (and Rza's brother) Mitchell "Divine" Diggs explained in a 2000 *Time* interview how the Clan even pioneered an innovative system of sharing recording budgets from solo record deals among the group's nine members, as each waited their turn for a solo release. "We did something that basically allows every family member to eat off every deal that we make. We did that because we knew that we had a lot of guys and, in a matter of eight years, it was going to be hard to get everyone's albums out based on, one, fan demand, and two, [the fact that] we had to find corporations willing to put up all that money to fund [nine solo record deals]," Divine explained. "So, we basically said if we've got X amount of dollars, we'll make sure that a large portion of that goes to the artist whose record it is, which may be Method Man or Inspectah Deck, but U-God and everyone else ate off of it, as well. They appeared on the records or whatever—but we found ways for everyone to get paid. And the same when the U-God album dropped. Others got paid in ways in which maybe [individual members] didn't see, but we see, because he's looking at whatever [this member] got [or that member] got, but we made plans for everyone to eat. That was the same system that was employed when he didn't have an album and Meth did [have] an album, the same system was employed when Raekwon did an album and Ghost didn't do an album. So, everyone kept the family bond and we put the bread on the table and everybody break[s] off their piece [to] eat and be merry."[215]

In that same 2000 *Time* interview, Divine explained the origin of this unique egalitarian setup by paralleling the Clan with the federal structure of the United States of America. "This model's been successful for eight years now. It has its ups and downs, don't get me wrong. But it's like the Constitution; we're not changing because a new administration wants to try different rules because of the times. The Constitution stands for all and forever," Divine explained.

When asked whether a new administration was synonymous with a successful solo career for any given Clan member, Divine agreed with that analogy. "Yeah, at that point [when any one member sees greater solo success than his fellow Clan members,] you may start to hear 'I don't want to be down no more, I'm taking [my] money and I'm leaving.' [The more successful solo member] doing that only hurts him[self]. Look at it like we are the United States and, if one state tries to break free, where are you going? What can you actually do without the help of the other states and without the nation standing by you? In the beginning, everyone in the Clan was represented by Wu-Tang in their solo deals. As they got older and more mature and thought they could learn things without us basically holding their hand, they went out and hired their own lawyers and their own accountants and their own agents. And that's what we want. [Those are] signs that this gentleman has learned after eight years what to do and how to manage himself. What me and RZA basically do is constantly keep them respecting the idea that 'maybe [that newly hired team] help[s] me out but [my fellow Wu-Tang members] are [the ones] really helping me out.'"[216]

Despite their generous equal division of publishing revenue (in addition to the sharing of solo recording budget money), there was no equal division of song appearances. Competition between Wu members to secure verses on *ETWT* is now legendary. Group member Masta Killa recalls in a 2006 interview, "You wouldn't ever have to try and push yourself, because if your shit wasn't right, it won't make the track."[217] Masta Killa, with far less rap experience than the other eight members, was only able to secure one verse on the debut album, on the closing verse of "Da Mystery of Chessboxin'."[218] The competition to secure verses on the album is made even clearer by the fact that Masta Killa recounted in a separate interview that "Da Mystery of Chessboxin'" was the last song recorded for *ETWT*, meaning that he barely made it on the album at all.[219]

It should be noted that this egalitarian agreement to evenly distribute publishing revenue did not always prevent monetary disputes from occurring. Over the years, Wu members have filed several lawsuits alleging financial discrepancies. Sixteen years after the release of *ETWT*, Ghostface sued Rza for unpaid publishing royalties and was awarded $151,255.18 in damages, in August 2009.[220] In an interview with *Wildstyle Mag* in Germany, Rza disputed that he owed Ghostface any money, even though he eventually lost the case at trial.[221]

"You know, when you make a Hip Hop song, fifty percent of the publishing goes to the producer of the music, and another fifty percent goes to the lyrics," Rza explained. "Ghost has a lawyer that says I should have only gotten twenty percent and that Ghost should have gotten more. So therefore they took all these times that I got fifty percent, added them up and said I owed them about 300 to 400 grand."[222]

Rza appealed the case after losing on the trial court level. The appellate court ruled that the trial court had utilized an incorrect method of calculating the damages, concluding that the trial court should lower the amount awarded to Ghostface.[223]

In 2008, U-God also sued Wu-Tang Productions, for $170,000, over unpaid royalties and appearance fees.[224] The contested amount was based on an alleged failure to pay U-God $40,000 in advance money for 2007 Wu-Tang album, *Eight Diagrams*, in addition to other alleged debts such as $50,000 purportedly owed to U-God for performances at the Rock The Bells concert series and an allegedly unpaid $60,000 publishing advance from a structured deal with BMG Music.

However, U-God went on to put his legal disagreement with Rza in a larger context. "One good memory was when Rza told me—I was still kinda wild and kinda crazy…and Rza sat down and told me, like, 'Yo, son, you gotta make a decision whether you gonna be in the streets or you gonna fuck with this Wu-Tang shit.' He sat me down like a fatherly figure," U-God revealed. "That's why I got the utmost respect for Rza to this day. We go through our little changes. This is business. You know what I'm saying? We go through our things, but deep down I love this nigga like…so fucking much for that talk. And he made me make a decision that changed my life."[225]

Outside Rza's guidance, U-God also learned lessons on his own. "Another thing I learned in this industry is that everything is contractual. You can't settle things in the street," said U-God in a recent interview. "You can't dig pockets if someone owes you money. You have to get a lawyer and go before the judge and get everything straightened out that way. And more importantly you have to move past it and keep business moving. A lot of people have bad blood. You cannot be emotional, though. This is business."[226]

Before the Wu-related lawsuits began, the Clan was more harmonious. Just four years after the release of their debut album, on the verge of the release of the Clan's second album, Inspectah Deck mused, "We're not dealing with the four devils—no envy, lust, greed, or hate. It's not about us [individually], it's [about] the Wu-Tang Clan."[227]

When asked in 2005 why he thought the Clan had been able to stay together so long, Rza's answer was succinct. "It's called The Wu-Tang Clan. And 'clan' means family," Rza said.

"Everything I do is Wu-Tang. Once I dedicated my life to that, I stayed firm to that."[228]

Chapter 7: God

The Nations of Gods and Earths (NGE) heavily influenced the Wu-Tang Clan and, by extension, influenced *ETWT* as well.

One of the ideas put forth by the NGE was breaking down the Latin alphabet into what they called The Supreme Alphabet, a coded system whereby each letter of the Latin alphabet signified a specific concept. The Supreme Alphabet is broken down below.

SUPREME ALPHABET

A = Allah

B = Be or Born

C = See (often spelled Cee)

D = Divine

E = Equality

F = Father

G = God

H = He (or Her)

I = Islam (or I)

J = Justice

K = King

L = Love, Hell or Right

M = Master

N = Now (also Nation or End)

O = Cipher (zero [0] in the Supreme Mathematics also signifies "cipher")

P = Power

Q = Queen

R = Ruler or Rule

S = Self-Savior

T = Truth (or Square, according to Rza)[229]

U = You or Universal

V = Victory

W = Wisdom (another word for Woman in NGE)

X = Unknown

Y = Why

Z = Zig Zag Zig (from the beginning to the end to the beginning)[230]

The Supreme Mathematics is NGE's system for assigning concepts to Arabic numerals. The concepts and numerals correspond as follows:

(1) Knowledge
(2) Wisdom
(3) Understanding
(4) Culture/Freedom
(5) Power/Refinement
(6) Equality
(7) GOD
(8) Build/Destroy
(9) Born
(0) Cipher[231]

———

The Supreme Alphabet recurs regularly throughout *ETWT*. In the second verse of "Clan In Da Front" when Gza says, "I'm on the mound, G," the "G" in that line is a Supreme Alphabet reference to "god."[232] On "Can It Be All So Simple," Raekwon's line "Back in the days of eight now" utilizes the Supreme Alphabet concept "now" ("N") as shorthand for nine (N-I-N-E or "now Islam now equality"), thus "eight now" references the year 1989 (8-9).

On the intro to "Wu-Tang: 7th Chamber," when Ghostface breathlessly describes how a Clan associate was gunned down and declares emphatically "I'm coming to get my culture cipher, god, then word is bond, crazy shots went the fuck off," he means that he got a forty ounce bottle of beer right before the shooting occurred (culture signifying "four" and cipher signifying "zero" in the Supreme Mathematics, thus 4-0 or forty).[233] It's only fitting that the skit leading into "Wu-Tang 7th Chamber" is the only skit on the album which contains a reference to the Supreme Mathematics. The song itself is the most NGE-influenced track on *ETWT*.

"7th Chamber" features seven verses from seven emcees. Several of the verses reference NGE philosophy. The Clan likely deliberately chose to have seven verses on the song (and to subtitle it "7th Chamber"), because seven signifies "god" in the Supreme Mathematics. God is also synonymous with the black man in NGE teachings.

The NGE references on the song take various forms. In the NGE tradition of creating new meanings for words by breaking them down into smaller parts, Raekwon refers to Wu-Tang by the acronym "We Usually Take All Niggas Garments" in his "7th Chamber" verse.[234] Inspectah Deck references Nation of Islam theology in his verse, by referring to the lost Tribe of Shabazz ("hit you with the force to leave you lost like the Tribe of Shabazz"). In the teachings of the Nation of Islam (adopted by NGE), Shabazz was the name of the tribe from which all humanity descended, the "lost" descriptor being added to refer specifically to the African-American descendants of this tribe who are lost "in the wilderness of North America."[235]

Rza utilizes the Supreme Alphabet to spell his name in the fifth verse, when he refers to himself as "Ruler Zig Zag Zig Allah." Ghostface closes his verse with the NGE's universal salutation "peace." Ol' Dirty Bastard closes his verse with a reference to his divine name, Ason Unique, and talks about dropping the "science" (dropping the science being an NGE phrase for utilizing the lessons of the NGE).[236]

The idea that "Wu-Tang: 7th Chamber" was designed around the concept of seven and its importance in the Supreme Mathematics is bolstered by later statements from Clan members regarding how the Supreme Mathematics influenced their records. For example, when asked how many tracks would appear on his forthcoming solo album, Dirty referenced the Supreme Mathematics. "Seventeen [tracks]. That's knowledge god being born to build and destroy. I'm not here to destroy; I'm only here to build. I got some shit that's gonna break down the devils and I got some shit that's gonna build up the gods and earths."[237]

NGE ideology appears on several other songs on the album. Ol' Dirty Bastard utilized an NGE reference in his first appearance on a record with the Clan. On "Protect Ya Neck," Dirty rapped "I'll be sticking pins in ya head like a fucking nurse," likely referencing what the 120 Lessons teach about the mad eugenicist Yacub, who had nurses stick pins and needles in the brains of black babies when they were born, in an attempt to assure that only lighter skinned babies would survive childbirth.[238] U-God closes his verse on "Da Mystery of Chessboxin" with a different reference to Yacub when he rapped that he was "making devils cower to the Caucus Mountains." The 120 Lessons teach that those mountains, more commonly referred to as the Caucasus Mountains, were the place where Yacub was driven into exile after he was chased from Mecca for his wicked ways.[239] In Ghostface's breakout verse on "Can It All Be So Simple," he rapped "the god left lessons on my dresser," referring to the 120 Lessons.

The influence of the NGE extends to the group's names as well. Group member U-God's stage name is an abbreviation of his divine name Universal God Allah ("U" stands for universal in the Supreme Alphabet).[240] As mentioned earlier, Rza's name in the Supreme Alphabet breaks down to Ruler Zig Zag Zig Allah. Gza's name breaks down to God Zig Zag Zig Allah.

Adherents to NGE have a general proclivity towards breaking down words into acronyms. In one pre-*ETWT* interview, Rza broke Wu-Tang down to "Wise Universal Truth Allah Now God" (its spelling in the Supreme Alphabet) and also mentioned two acronyms for the group name that were both later referenced in their music: "We Usually Take All Niggas Garments" and "Witty Unpredictable Talent And Natural Game."[241] "C.R.E.AM." is the most famous acronym on *ETWT*, breaking down to Cash Rules Everything Around Me.[242]

Beyond traditional NGE teachings, there is also a more traditional Islamic and occasional Arabic influence on Wu-Tang—as is to be expected, since Islam had an influence on NGE.[243] For example, Raekwon sometimes goes by Shallah ("of God" in Arabic). Masta Killa also goes by the Arabic name Jamel Arief (Jamel being Arabic for "handsome,"[244] while Arief means "wise").[245] On "Can It All Be So Simple," Raekwon references Medina. Medina is known as the second holiest city in Islam, but NGE adherents use Medina as the divine name for the borough of Brooklyn, in New York City (which itself has the divine name "Now Why," in the Supreme Alphabet).[246]

The "36 Chambers" part of the full *ETWT* album title also had significance in the NGE system of thought. During an interview, Method Man explained how the "36 Chambers" part of the title expanded beyond the obvious martial arts film reference and connected to the group's NGE philosophy. "There's thirty-six fatal points on the body, right?" Meth began his explanation to journalist Cheo Coker, referring to the fighting philosophy espoused in the film *The 36th Chamber of Shaolin*. "[Those fatal points are] ten degrees apart. When you multiply all that, you get 360, the perfect cycle."[247] The concept of three hundred and sixty degrees is important to adherents of NGE, who stand in a circle (which is 360 degrees) called a "cipher" when discussing ("building on") the mathematical and scientific concepts they learn as part of NGE.

The impact of NGE on the lives and outlook of the members of the Clan long predates the recording of *ETWT*. Raekwon said he got knowledge of self (i.e. became aware of the teachings of the Nation of Gods and Earths) in 1987.[248] Ghostface said he gained knowledge of self in 1985 through his brother's uncle.[249] Cappadonna recalled getting knowledge of self in 1986 or 1987.[250] Masta Killa credited long-time Wu-Tang DJ Allah Mathematics as one of the key individuals who taught him the 120 Lessons.[251]

Knowing the lessons, however, is not the same as considering oneself a part of the Nation of Gods and Earths. In a 2004 interview with online media outlet *AllHipHop.com*, Ghostface shocked an interviewer by revealing that he never belonged to the Five Percent Nation, another name by which the Nation of Gods and Earths is known. "I'm not a part of the Five Percent Nation. I always respected what the brothers spoke about, but I was never a part of it," Ghostface stated. "I respect the lessons and all that. I agreed with a lot of their ideology."[252] In the same interview, Ghostface revealed that he is a practitioner of Islam.

Christianity also influenced the Clan. "There is a book in the Bible, in Revelation, that says, 'In the last days, the Son of Man will come. And out of his mouth will come a double-edged sword. And with this sword, he shall smite the nations.' To me, I said, 'That's us, yo. We're men, we're the son of men, and out of our mouths, our tongue is our sword.' A sword can't [literally] come out of a man's mouth, but your tongue is shaped like a sword. And with this [tongue], we're going to rock the world," Rza reflected.[253]

The particular biblical verse to which Rza was referring, Revelation 1:16, was a description of how Jesus would appear when he returned to Earth, as revealed to John.[254] Of particular importance to adherents to NGE, the Messiah is also described in that chapter as holding seven stars. In the same chapter, John is instructed to give the word of the impending return of Christ to "seven churches" (verse 11) and he sees "seven golden lampshades" (verse 12) before he sees Christ himself.[255] The recurrence of the number seven throughout this chapter must have particularly struck Rza, since the number seven has divine importance in the teachings of NGE, as a number that is representative of god.

Central to NGE science is the idea that the black man is god in the flesh. Christian teachings proclaim that Jesus was God in the flesh,[256] thus it was likely particularly important to Rza that, in this same chapter of Revelation, Jesus is described as having hair "like wool" (verse 14) and "feet like bronze" (verse 15), lines that have led some scholars to infer that Jesus was a black man (bronze skinned, with woolen hair).[257]

On the other hand, the Clan also turned a critical eye towards some Christian teachings in their music. Matthew 5:39 proclaims "But I say to you, do not resist an evil person; but whoever slaps you on your right cheek, turn the other to him also." [258] Rza dismisses this "turning the other cheek" philosophy on his "Protect Ya Neck" verse, by rapping "turn the other cheek and I'll break your fucking chin."

An argument could be made that the teachings of NGE about the inherent godliness of black men is what gave Clan members the confidence to believe that they could achieve success in the music business, despite their hectic upbringing. Evidence of how the teachings of the NGE ("knowledge of self") may have inspired the Clan is demonstrated by the work ethic that Clan members displayed from a young age. Near the time that Rza acquired knowledge of self, he got hired for his first job, while he was still an elementary school student. "I had my first job at the age of 11, selling newspapers on the Verrazano Bridge," Rza told one Canadian interviewer. "I would have to stand in traffic and sell it. I would make about ten dollars, twelve dollars a day. At the end of the week, I'd have sixty, seventy bucks. That was enough to buy a pair of Pumas, some Lees, and give some money to [my family to] help my mother out."[259]

Beyond giving him the confidence to pursue an entrepreneurial path by teaching him about his innate righteous nature, Rza attributes the lessons of the NGE with an even deeper significance. "To know the ledge, so you don't fall off the edge, into the devil's civilization, is vitally important. For me, it saved my life," Rza said, when addressing the importance of the lessons taught by the Nation of Gods and Earths to his life.[260] One should also note here how Rza, in NGE tradition, breaks down the word "knowledge" to "know the ledge" ("know[ing] the ledge" is NGE shorthand for having "knowledge of self").

Knowing the ledge, however, involves more than knowing what one learns from the NGE. The Nation of Gods and Earths also fills their adherents with a general thirst for knowledge, particularly from literature. "I loved reading books. I grew up reading a lot. Reading was important to me. I didn't really have a hundred percent proper education," Raekwon said, when asked if he enjoyed reading books. "When we started getting into [the] Five Percent Nation, it was always about reading, though. Reading was definitely something fundamental to me. If you didn't read, you didn't know how to write."[261]

In that same spirit of acquiring knowledge in order to write well, Gza has spent the past few years meeting with astrophysicists around the country, to research his next album, tentatively titled *Dark Matter*, which will delve into the physics of dark matter.[262] While interviewing Gza about the *Dark Matter* project, physicist (and current *Cosmos* host) Neil deGrasse Tyson took a moment to read a Facebook posting left on his page by a Wu fan named Michael Rafales, who recounted how the Clan ignited his love of science. "As a teenager, it was not my school, it was Wu-Tang, that taught me the idea of knowledge, wisdom and understanding," Rafales wrote. "It was because of this idea that I went into physics. I am now a high school science teacher with a passion for sharing my love of science and improving scientific literacy."[263]

This desire to teach reflects the NGE tenet stating that their adherents, the Five Percent, are poor righteous teachers, a title which implicitly encourages NGE adherents to *spread* the knowledge they attain.[264] In that spirit, twenty years after the release of *ETWT*, Gza has partnered with science educators for a program named Science Genius, which Gza describes as "a project I've been involved with where high school students compete in rap battles where the subject is science."[265] He went on to say, "Raps will be based on natural selection, for example. It's a way to get kids more involved with science through music."[266]

Poor righteous teachers, indeed.

Chapter 8: Build and Destroy

Without Rza, the circumstances surrounding the Wu-Tang Clan could have destroyed them before they became a group at all. Rza and Ghostface grew up in Stapleton and roughly half of the Clan grew up in Park Hill (Raekwon, Inspectah Deck, Method Man, and U-God). In one interview, Rza explained how, near the time of the Wu's formation, Stapleton and Park Hill were warring with one another and his household was neutral ground, where even sworn enemies in the neighborhood rivalry could sit side by side.[267]

Not everyone in the Wu remembers the rivalry being as intense as Rza did. In a 2005 article with *thefader.com*, Ghostface's memory of the rivalry was slightly different. As he recalled, the rivalry had ended by the time Wu-Tang formed and no one in the Wu clashed with any fellow member during the rivalry.[268]

Although Ghostface does not recall any acts of neighborhood-related violence being committed amongst the Wu, at least one researcher has uncovered an incident where Ghostface was indeed involved in the neighborhood rivalry, although not in an incident involving a fellow Clan member. In *The Big Payback*, author Dan Charnas recounts a story where, allegedly, at one point when neighborhood tensions were boiling, Ghostface Killah (a Stapleton resident) shot up the home of future

Wu business manager, Power, who lived in Park Hill.[269]

Memories also diverge on the matter of Ghost and Raekwon's early relationship. Ghost shared in one interview his recollection of going to school with Raekwon (who lived in Park Hill), but couldn't recall saying much more to him than a greeting in passing.[270] According to longtime Clan father figure Poppa Wu and Rza, Ghostface's early relationship with Raekwon was more complicated than merely greeting each other in passing. Without implicating anyone specifically, Poppa Wu recalled Raekwon being with Power when Ghostface's house was shot up.[271] In a *LA Times* interview, Rza recalled that Raekwon (from Park Hill) and Ghostface (from Stapleton) held enmity towards one another before the Clan formed. "Raekwon and Ghostface started off as enemies in the neighborhood," Rza recalled. "They grew to be best friends after joining the Wu-Tang."[272] Beyond friendship, both men would eventually form a musical bond so deep, it enabled them to create the song that was arguably the emotional centerpiece of *ETWT*: "Can It Be All So Simple."

The chemistry between Ghostface and Raekwon was not an accident, however, but was illustrative of an overall sonic plan that Wu members had for the group sound. At the Red Bull Music Academy, Raekwon and Ghostface spoke on how Wu-Tang was deliberately patterned after New York hardcore rap collective,

The Hit Squad.[273] They noted that the idea of pairing Raekwon and Ghostface on the classic *ETWT* single "Can It Be All So Simple" was inspired by the chemistry exhibited by EPMD, the founders of the Hit Squad.[274]

However, the chemistry between Clan members actually predates the first EPMD record. "The style that we've got can't be duplicated or imitated, because it dates back to chemistry we've had since 1986," said Method Man when discussing the Clan's unique sound in a 1994 interview.[275]

Chemistry between Clan members also influenced how individual members built their respective styles. In an interview with online media outlet *Halftime*, Inspectah Deck revealed that he crafted his low-key vocal and personal style to stand in contrast to the more frenetic styles of fellow Clansmen such as Ol' Dirty Bastard and Rza.[276]

The unique styles of the Clan may also have been influenced by their past experiences with other elements of hip-hop culture. In an interview with online media outlet *AllHipHop*, Inspectah Deck discussed how he was a graffiti artist known as Rebel INS, in his formative years, long before the Clan started.[277] Rza used to write graffiti under the name Razor.[278] The first element U-God practiced was beatboxing, backing up longtime Clan affiliate Cappadonna.[279]

In another interview, Deck revealed that he and Ghostface both had a background in breaking. "I used to breakdance. I used to pop and lock. I used to battle Ghostface Killah. Ghostface Killah used to breakdance, I used to pop and lock, Electric Boogie. We used to go to junior high school together. We used to just battle every day like it was *Beat Street*, the movie…Ghostface used to have an Afro, like the Jackson 5. He used to do windmills," said Deck.[280]

It's unclear how the practice of these disparate elements of hip-hop culture influenced the formation of the Clan's unique rap styles. Still, one can almost envision (for example) Ghostface's unique approach to flowing over a beat as being influenced by his background in breaking, a form of physical artistry that enhances the rhythmic understanding of music of its practitioners. Along this same line of thought, Rza mentioned Method Man's dancing background in *The Wu-Tang Manual* and expressed his belief that a background in dance could indeed have an influence on one's MC style. "[Meth] was always like a Michael Jackson dancing nigga back in the day. And when he's on the mic, it still sounds like he's dancing," Rza stated.[281]

One thing that practitioners of all these disparate hip-hop elements have in common is a disdain for imitation, derisively known as "biting."[282] Following this credo, the Clan took protecting their style from duplication by others very seriously. In one interview, Inspectah Deck related a story about how Ol' Dirty Bastard confronted a rapper named Akinyele about having a style he felt was too similar to his own, snatching the mic from Akinyele's hand during one of his performances.[283] In the "Shark Niggas (Biters)" skit on Raekwon's solo debut, *Only Built 4 Cuban Linx*, Ghost warned ominously, "I don't want no nigga sounding like me on no album!"[284]

They were likely so protective of their style because it took them so long to perfect it. Part of perfecting one's craft involves being deeply self-critical. Even after years of rhyming, at least one member of the Clan described his rapping ability as a work in progress, during the time *ETWT* was recorded. "Even when we did *Enter The 36 Chambers*, I didn't consider myself a great emcee, I [just] considered myself good," Raekwon said humbly of his ability when the recording of *ETWT* began.[285] "I was still finding myself as a writer."

However, Raekwon believed that his writing improved rapidly over the course of recording *ETWT*. When asked later about the moment when he felt he wrote something special, Raekwon singled out his now-legendary performance on the biggest single from *ETWT*: "C.R.E.A.M."

"It was the 'C.R.E.A.M.' record that really touched me, because that's a true story: coming from Brooklyn to Staten Island and seeing my mom being a single mother. It wasn't a beat you could brag on, it was a beat that I felt deserved a story. I could picture myself as a kid, eating a $100,000 bar. I didn't write about my life at first." At this point in his recollection, Raekwon admitted that the initial reaction to this early version of "C.R.E.A.M." from one (unnamed) Clan member was that Raekwon needed to write a personal story, not a general one. "I don't want to hear no [imaginary] stories, I want to hear where we come from," Raekwon remembers his Clan partner saying. "It was eight to one. He was the only one questioning it." Still, that one dissenting vote led Raekwon to change his verse. This anecdote succinctly embodies the strength of the Clan's brotherhood and how much even a solitary dissenting voice was valued amongst the family of nine.[286]

As serious as their music often was, the Wu also occasionally exhibited a keen sense of humor. A great example of this is the "Torture" skit, which featured Method Man and Raekwon playfully describing different ways to hypothetically torture one another.[287] Comic interplay between Method Man and Raekwon can also be found in a somewhat humorous exchange about the whereabouts of Raekwon's VHS copy of *The Killer*, in the skit that opens "Wu-Tang 7th Chamber."

The "Torture" skit aside, the violence of Wu's upbringing is generally explored in a more serious fashion on *ETWT*. Despite its light-hearted opening, the skit preceding "Wu-Tang:

7th Chamber" is largely dominated by Ghostface Killah entering the scene to announce that one of the Clan's associates has just been murdered, emphasizing the treacherous nature of the surroundings in which they were raised. As if the war zone-like atmosphere of the Clan's section of Staten Island wasn't apparent, when the skit ends, the song begins with one Clan member bellowing the "Good Morning Vietnam" greeting that Robin Williams made famous in the war film *Good Morning Vietnam*.[288]

In addition to the specter of violence, the upbringing of the Clan was mired in poverty. "I come from welfare checks and food stamps," Rza explained in a 1997 *Spin* interview. "There was literally a day when you could ask for a quarter and not get it." Then, to illustrate the point even more clearly, he added, "[You might] have to borrow five dollars from somebody else's mother, and that five dollars will buy you a pound of bologna, a loaf of bread, not even some milk—maybe you might get something to drink, a packet of Kool-Aid."[289]

The Clan's early economic limitations unexpectedly might have helped solidify the leadership position of Rza. "Everything started in Rza's basement. We didn't have money for a studio," Raekwon recalled of the group's humble origins.[290]

That same economic deprivation also tightened the bond between Clan members and their respective families, as each member and their closest relatives all worked together to help the Clan move forward. "Raekwon's mother, she was the cook. She used to sell dinners in the hood for $5, so she was feeding us," Inspectah Deck recalled, thinking back on how not just the Clan, but even their family members, supported the effort of recording *ETWT*. "RZA's mother was helping us take care of our financial things as his partner at the time. It was more of a family thing."[291]

In addition to employing assistance from their family members, group members themselves handled multiple responsibilities to assure that the group as a whole succeeded, as exemplified by Masta Killa's recollection of the Clan's first live performance. "I ain't perform that night, but I gave everybody they *haircuts*. Then we went state to state, [in a] 12-passenger van, somebody always slobbering on your shoulder. I didn't perform every night, but they needed a driver. It was all about winning."[292]

In an interview with *XXL*, Deck explained that the tight bond the Clan shares goes far beyond the music industry. "We didn't come together to make a record. We were already together…if the record didn't happen, we still would be as tight as we are."[293]

The close knit familial spirit of the Clan and the rapid success of *ETWT* alone were not enough to shield the friends and family of the

Clan from the destructive forces in the environment from which they emerged. Just four months after the album's release, Clan member U-God's two-year-old son, Dante Hawkins, was wounded when he was caught in the crossfire of a shootout in Stapleton.[294] Days later, two other people close to Wu were shot: Darryl Routte and 2 Cent. Routte, the brother of Guy Routte (who managed Clan affiliate Shyheim), was shot and wounded in an argument.[295] More tragically, Clan affiliate 2 Cent was shot and killed.[296]

2 Cent would later be memorialized in a graffiti mural ("R.I.P. 2 Cent") that appears at the 0:57 mark of the "Can It All Be So Simple" video.[297] At the 4:26 mark of the same video, a glimpse can be seen of a larger mural, with the words "Can It All Be So Simple" in huge letters in its center, that memorializes the deaths of 2 Cent and another Wu affiliate named Kase, who was killed by a police officer.[298]

Despite the string of tragedies affecting the Clan's family and friends, their music was still undeniably successful and their success was building daily. In April 1994, within weeks of when the tragedies described above occurred, *ETWT* was certified gold for sales of half a million copies and "C.R.E.A.M." was holding strong in the top 20 on *Billboard's* Hot Rap Singles chart.[299] "C.R.E.A.M." was also number one on the maxi-single sales chart for Hot Dance Music in early April.[300] This ranking would place "C.R.E.A.M." above singles by superstars of that era, such as Snoop Doggy Dogg ("Gin and Juice") and R. Kelly ("Bump-n-Grind"). On the other hand, "C.R.E.A.M," at #80, ranked well below both singles (at #2 and #9, respectively) on the Hot 100 chart (ranked according to a combination of sales and radio airplay of singles).[301] Apparently, "C.R.E.A.M" outsold both singles that week, but received far less radio airplay than either.

Although the Clan never expressed animosity towards the West Coast, the radio support West Coast rap singles like Snoop's "Gin and Juice" received—contrasted with lower airplay for East Coast rap singles like "C.R.E.A.M."—might explain some of the coastal animosity expressed by other East Coast artists of that era.[302] Instead of engaging in coastal animosity, the Clan was congenial with West Coast artists, as their aforementioned inclusion of West Coast rap veteran MC Eiht in the "Can It All Be So Simple" video illustrated. The love for the Clan was reciprocated by West Coast-based artists. For example, Method Man was the only New York rapper featured on 2Pac's 1996 album *All Eyez on Me*, released in the middle of his war of words with New York-based label, Bad Boy Records.[303]

As testimony to the love the Clan received regardless of geography, the group would go on to record their second album, *Wu-Tang Forever*, in Los Angeles, staying there for months after The Notorious B.I.G. was murdered in L.A. on March

9, 1997. There is no record of the group facing any problems during their stay there.

Chapter 9: Born

There are many factors that led to the birth of the Wu-Tang Clan. There are also factors that might have prevented them from forming into the nine-man group we know today. One of the factors that could have stopped the Clan from forming is if either Gza or Rza would have been successful in their solo careers, before the Clan was formed.

Rza, rhyming as Prince Rakeem, didn't experience much commercial success with his debut single, "Ooh, I Love You Rakeem." When reflecting on the single in an interview, over ten years after it was released, Rza remembered the song as being driven by show business politics, although he admits that it had autobiographical qualities. "That was more label-directed. I did it, but it wasn't like [I wasn't] being me. I definitely love women, and that rap was a true story, too. Every girl I named was a girlfriend at one point, and some of them were my girlfriend[s] at the same time when I did that song," Rza recalled.[304]

Although the decision to feature a bevy of ladies repeating "Ooh, I Love You Rakeem" in the hook and the song's content might have made it seem commercial, the track also featured the hard drums for which Rza would later become known, to assure the song had at least some hardcore appeal. It might surprise some Wu fans to discover that Prince Paul crafted those hard drums, not Rza—even though Rza was credited as the song's producer, under his then-alias Prince Rakeem.[305]

In one interview, Rza recounted how, beyond just assisting with the drum programming on "Ooh I Love You, Rakeem," Prince Paul also taught him some production techniques. "Prince Paul was one of the first producers and people who helped me in the whole music industry. Back when I did 'Ooh I Love You Rakeem', he did the drums in it. The high-hats. He schooled me on that. He schooled me on a lot of things. I did a lot of demos with him in those days," Rza recounted.[306]

In addition to the hard drums on its A-side, Rza took another precaution to assure his debut single would satisfy the hardcore rap fans he sought to reach, by assuring that the B-side songs on the "Ooh, I Love You, Rakeem" single had a more rugged style.[307] "That was just one song on an album full of hardcore stuff. In those days, hip-hop albums always had one R&B song or one reggae song or one love song. My album was like that, too. I had a lot of hardcore stuff. I had stories. Basically, what happened was, 'Ooh I Love You Rakeem' was the single that I got signed for to Tommy Boy, but they weren't sure they were going to do an album. I had a single deal with an album option. Even though the single wasn't exactly in my vein, I thought, 'Okay, let me do the single, but let me pen two or three songs on the B-side.' So for the same price, they got all that music, which made it basically an EP, but it was only a single deal. The reason I did that was because I didn't want 'Ooh I Love You Rakeem' to be the only portrayal of me."[308]

Aside from adding hardcore appeal to the single, the songs Rza included on its B-side would serve as a harbinger of his work with the Clan and displayed the influence martial arts films had on him. One of the B-side cuts, a remix of a track called "Sexcapades," was subtitled "Wu-Tang Mix."[309] The title of another B-side cut that Rza produced, "Deadly Venoms," also foreshadowed the influence that martial arts cinema would have on his future work (*Five Deadly Venoms* being the title of a classic martial arts film).[310] Thus, even as early as 1991, when the single was released, Rza was incorporating martial arts film references—including the name Wu-Tang—into his work.

Despite all the careful planning Rza put into constructing his first commercial release, we will never know whether Rza's solo career would have taken off based on his debut single, because any commercial success that record might have achieved was cut short when Rza was arrested. Instead of getting bailed out by his record label, Tommy Boy, Rza was instead dropped from the label.[311]

Like his cousin Rza, Gza also did not see much success with his solo debut. Unlike Rza, Gza was actually able to release a full length album—not just a single—on Cold Chillin'

Records, a legendary record label that released classic albums from Big Daddy Kane, Biz Markie, Kool G Rap, and the rest of the Juice Crew. Despite (or perhaps because of) this heavyweight roster, Gza received little promotion when his album, *Words From The Genius*, was released.[312] Brooklyn hip-hop veteran Easy Mo' Bee produced ten of the fifteen tracks on *Words From The Genius*. Three years later, Easy Mo' Bee would produce six tracks on *Ready to Die*, the acclaimed debut album from Brooklyn MC, The Notorious BIG.[313] Gza's solo debut only sold a fraction of what *Ready to Die* did, but perhaps this was for the greater good, as it is unclear whether Gza would have been a part of the Wu-Tang Clan, if he had attained solo success with *Words From The Genius*.

Potential solo success for Rza or Gza was not the only variable that could have altered the Wu as we know it. Several narrowly averted tragedies could have changed the group's lineup dramatically, if history went a different way. In a CNN interview, Rza described the day when his decision to call Method Man over to him from across the street inadvertently allowed Meth to escape being shot and possibly killed (another victim standing nearby was not so lucky).[314]

Unexpectedly, this near-death experience for Method Man also demonstrated the depth of the Clan's devotion to Rza. "Meth, he always brings it up...that [on] that day [I] saved his life. He actually said, if it was anybody else calling him, he wouldn't have [crossed the street]," Rza recalled.[315] It would be hard to imagine the Clan without Meth, especially considering the fact that the song "Method Man" was so key to the Wu's early success.

Another lucky near-miss that could have derailed the Clan's formation was Rza's 1991 acquittal on felonious assault charges.[316] "It was the victory over that incident that made me change my whole direction. In a way, it's [a] double-edged [sword] in that incident. One, if I would've lost that, yeah, Wu-Tang wouldn't have happened, but also it's the victory [over] it that inspired me and gave me the drive also to go and really get serious about Wu-Tang," Rza recalled in an interview, years after the fact.[317]

The Clan could have lost another key member near the same time as Rza's trial, when Ghostface was purportedly shot in the neck, in the same Ohio town (Steubenville) where Rza beat his felonious assault charge.[318] The Ghostface shooting incident, which could easily have proven fatal, was a pivotal moment to which Method Man referred cryptically, in a later interview, as a sacrifice for the whole group to attain success. "A lot of people sacrificed a lot for us to get to where we are," Method Man said, recalling the early days of the Clan. "Ghostface took bullets in the neck for this shit."[319] Meth did not elaborate further.

The Steubenville shooting incident may have been re-enacted in Ghostface's verse on the "Can It All Be So Simple" remix, released on

Raekwon's solo debut *Only Built 4 Cuban Linx*, where Ghost rapped "Stumbling, holding my neck, to the god's rest/Opened flesh, burgundy blood colored my Guess/Emergency, trauma, black teen headed for surgery/Can it be? An out of state nigga tried to murder me." The reference to "holding my neck" (presumptively because he was shot there) and the shooter being from "out of state" (shorthand for a person not from New York), raise the inference that the Steubenville shooting was being described in that verse.

Raekwon recounted the earliest and most potentially tragic near miss that could have forever altered the Clan's future, by describing a childhood incident between him and U-God. "When we was little, we were playing with guns," Raekwon recalled. "We [were] young and shit, we [were] at Cappa's house. Next thing you know, [we're] playing with it, kept loading it. Next thing, U[-God]...pointed it at me...I was like 'Don't point that at me' and U pointed it towards the window and 'blaow', it went off. The kid could've been outta here."[320]

There are other ways the group makeup could have been altered. Before Wu-Tang existed, Wu members belonged to several smaller groups. Rza, Gza and Ol' Dirty Bastard formed the All In Together crew. Inspectah Deck, U-God and Method Man formed a group together.[321] Method Man, Raekwon, and Inspectah Deck also had a group they called DMD Crew (short for Dick 'Em Down).[322] Any one of these smaller groups could have decided not to follow Rza's vision to form the larger Wu-Tang Clan, forever altering the chemistry we now hear in their classic debut album. To give credence to this concept of the possibility of separate smaller sub-groups being formed, instead of the Clan as the world knows it, consider that despite the extensive MC experience of each respective Wu member, they apparently never performed together as the nine man group we now know as Wu before "Protect Ya Neck" was recorded. Or, at least, that seems to be the case based on a recent quote from U-God regarding the first Wu performance.

"The first [Wu-Tang Clan] show, probably about ten people [were] in there. And the microphone was hooked up to a stereo," U-God recalled with a laugh. "This was down South, in North Carolina, when we started doing a promo tour. We had to perform in front of ten people like they were 10,000 people."[323] Like many stories involving the early days of the Clan, recollections regarding key events vary. Masta Killa recalls the first Wu show differently than U-God. His version seems more probable, as he recalls that show occurring in New York City, the group's hometown (where they were more likely to perform first than in North Carolina). "The first Wu show actually was in East New York, at the Showboat," Masta Killa recalled, in a separate interview.[324]

As opposed to fewer members, the Clan also could have had more members. Potential tenth Wu member Cappadonna mentioned in an interview that he was imprisoned from the period when *ETWT* was recorded until recording sessions began for Raekwon's solo debut, *Only Built For Cuban Linx*, thus preventing him from becoming the tenth member of Wu.[325] However, Cappadonna still had an indirect effect on the final line-up in the group, as U-God has credited Cappadonna with inspiring him to become a hip-hop artist. "I started rhyming [in] like 1985," U-God recalled. "Cappadonna was the one who got me rhyming."[326] In a separate interview with *Vice*, U-God also revealed he was introduced to the rest of the Clan by Cappadonna.[327]

Shockingly, one Wu affiliate's inability to stay awake also affected who wound up in the Wu. In an interview, Killah Priest revealed that the only reason why Masta Killa appeared on *ETWT* instead of him is because Priest fell asleep during the recording of "Da Mystery of Chessboxin'."[328]

In one hypothetical scenario that may have derailed the completion of *ETWT*, the Clan might not have even closed their iconic deal with Loud Records, as Loud founder Steve Rifkind recalled that Rza was very difficult to locate during the time he wanted to sign the Clan. "Rza, I had been trying to track him down forever. He didn't have an answering machine or anything."[329] Luckily, Rza found Rifkind. "He just showed up one day. It was my birthday, my 31st birthday. I was with E-Swift from The Alkaholiks. [Rza] didn't have the ["Protect Ya Neck"] record, so he brought the whole Clan to perform the record [live]. I don't know if this guy was an intern, but somebody came in and said 'That's that shit!' while they were performing. I never saw that guy again," Rifkind recalls. When asked if the intern's opinion was persuasive, Rifkind responded in the affirmative. "It was a done deal. The deal was done a week later."[330]

The treachery inherent in living the street life nearly played a part in changing the final lineup for the Wu. Imprisonment almost deprived the group of one of their core nine members, as U-God only just made it onto *ETWT*, due to being imprisoned for much of the recording process for the album.[331] U-God came home on parole to add minimal vocals to *ETWT*, then was imprisoned again after the album was completed.[332]

Imprisonment also ironically may have aided the Clan as well. Rza was given access to production equipment by RNS, a producer for The UMC's, a Staten Island rap group that pre-dated Wu, during RNS' incarceration.[333] Specifically, RNS provided Rza with the EPS on which Rza produced pre-Clan beats for individual Wu members, well before the prospect of any group record deal.[334] Subsequently, Rza used the EPS machine to create a significant number of the beats that appeared on *ETWT*.[335]

"I ran into my man RNS, who [later] produced Shyheim's album," Rza recalled. "He was going through financial problems, and I was making a little street money…he had to go away for a while, so I lent him some money and he let me hold his EPS. Boom! Deck, Meth, [and] U-God used to come over [to] the lab all the time. Ghostface used to live with me at the time, and you know that Ol' Dirty and GZA are my cousins, so we all were making tapes…RNS left it there about 90 days."[336]

Without RNS being imprisoned, Rza might not have gained access to this key piece of equipment. Having access to RNS' equipment also helped solidify Rza as the central figure in the Wu, as the other members would regularly come to his house to rhyme over beats he created with his newly acquired equipment. "We would go up to Rza's house, he would throw on beats and we would freestyle," Raekwon explained.[337] This opportunity to rhyme together frequently also likely helped sharpen the now-legendary chemistry between Clan members on the microphone.

Chapter 10: Knowledge Cipher

Place and geography is hugely important in hip-hop. In the genre's beginning stages, MC's would get parties in a frenzy by calling out different neighborhoods. As hip-hop spread from the Bronx, the boroughs of Brooklyn, Manhattan (Uptown) and Queens would all earn their party shoutouts.[338] Staten Island was the borough that was often left out. Wu-Tang Clan aimed to fill that void. "We started to raise a stake for Staten Island. When you come from a borough that nobody…mentions when you're going out, when you're hanging out and they think something's sweet? It was like a revenge move to get...on," Raekwon recounted, at the Red Bull Music Academy.[339]

Rza's early travels throughout New York City became informal market research on how to craft music that would win the heart of his hometown. These journeys also expanded Rza's vision about what was possible in his life, far beyond the confines of the housing projects where he was raised. "Growing up in New York, there are a lot of tenement buildings and a lot of projects. You don't leave your projects too much," Rza recounted. "The laundry's there, the grocery store is there. Everything takes place right there. When I got knowledge of myself and thought about moving around the city, hip-hop was something that helped me. With hip-hop, I had to move around just to hear it, because it wasn't everywhere. You had to go to the Bronx."[340]

The international appeal of the Clan can also partially be attributed to Rza and Ghost's early decision to name the Clan after a group based a world away from them, in the province of Hubei, located in southern central China.[341] Although the Clan likely was unaware of the English translation of Shaolin when they chose that as a nickname for Staten Island, it's interesting in retrospect to note that Shaolin translates into "youthful forest."[342] This "youthful forest" translation is ironic considering how two attributes—a disproportionately high youth population and metaphors like "urban jungle"—are associated with the housing project environment in which the Wu-Tang was raised, an environment which they would come to call Shaolin ("youthful forest"). The Wudang Mountains, in which the Wu-Tang Clan of martial arts film lore resides, is ironically also referred to as Wudangshan on Chinese maps (ironic in the sense that Wudangshan appears so similar to the name Wu-Tang Clan).[343] The irony continues further, as the first house of worship constructed for the monks of Wu-Tang was built during the Tang Dynasty.[344]

Coincidences in terms of places connected to the Wu-Tang Clan do not end there. As an interesting precursor to Rza's own entrepreneurial ascent, his Stapleton neighborhood was also home to one of the most successful entrepreneurs in American history. Almost 200 years before Rza was born, Stapleton was where wealthy industrialist Cornelius Vanderbilt grew up, on a farm.[345] Decades later, farming would be foreign to the urbanized environment of the housing projects eventually built in Stapleton. At eight stories high, those projects, formally referred to as Stapleton Houses, are the largest housing projects on Staten Island.[346] In their youth, the height of the Stapleton Houses may have allowed Rza and Ghostface to look across the Lower Bay to Brooklyn, just across the water from them and the home borough to Rza's cousins Gza and Ol' Dirty Bastard.[347]

Although other housing projects prominently associated with hip-hop, such as the Magnolia Projects in New Orleans, have been re-developed over the years, the projects where the Clan was raised remain virtually unchanged and can be visited today.[348] Ghostface was recently interviewed in front of the place where he grew up, Building 218 in the Stapleton Houses development, which still looks the same as it did in the Clan-related videos where it has appeared.[349]

The neighborhood surrounding Stapleton Houses is more nuanced and complex than one might gather merely by listening to the Clan's music. The middle school across the street from the Stapleton Houses, Berta A. Dreyfus Intermediate School 49, is far from the stereotype associated with an "inner city school," as it offers special magnet programming for gifted students.[350] Additionally, Stapleton was the site of a planned (but never completed) naval base, the construction for which began in 1983 and stalled in 1993, right before Stapleton gave the world its greatest export: the Wu-Tang Clan.[351]

Staten Island was where the Clan was born, but after they completed their first cipher of knowledge (passed the age of ten), that's when they truly began to build the character they needed to start an empire. That character building began with the Clan's early work experiences. Before he was the star of the group, Method Man was one of the hardest working members of the Clan. In the years before the Clan would shake up the music world, Method Man worked at the Statue of Liberty, a job that not only was likely to have enabled him to broaden his cultural horizons by interacting with a broad range of people from around the world, but also led to him meeting Dan Smalls, a former Statue of Liberty co-worker with Meth who (years later) would play him the music of The Notorious B.I.G. for the first time.[352] Over the course of five years, Meth worked his way up to an assistant manager position at the Statue of Liberty.[353]

Method Man wasn't the only Clan member whose early work experience would lay the foundation for the strong work ethic that he would later apply to his musical endeavors. Most likely as a result of the challenges they faced growing up, the Clan seemed determined to work their way out of poverty, from a young age. Rza included future Clan members in his entrepreneurial activities even in his early teenage years. "When I was 13, I had a job as a fruit peddler," Rza recalled. "Me and ODB would get up early in the morning. We'd go and unload apples, oranges and peaches, put them in a fruit stand in downtown Brooklyn, and sell all day. Or [we'd get paid to] give out flyers. We made about eighty-five bucks a week....that was enough to buy our own pants and our own sneakers."[354]

Including Rza's elementary school experience selling newspapers and fruit (alongside ODB), his work history continued from age 11 almost up to his entry into the music business. "When I became 15, I had summer jobs. I would be cleaning up the park, cleaning up the pool, being a pool night watchman," Rza said, reminiscing on his early work history. "One of my worst jobs, I worked in a factory. I would [sort] screws and nuts and put them in a box. A monkey could do this...this job was right next to a pepper factory, so I was sneezing all day."[355]

Masta Killa was no stranger to menial labor as a youth either, as hardcore East Coast rapper Jeru The Damaja recently revealed in an interview that he worked as a teenager alongside Masta Killa at a McDonald's.[356] Like Rza, Ghostface also had a job selling newspapers as a youth and would later also land a job bagging groceries, followed by assorted summer youth jobs involving landscaping.[357] Inspectah Deck worked as a bike messenger in Manhattan.[358] A year before *ETWT* was recorded, U-God was in his second year of college, studying to become a mortician.[359]

Furthermore, Method Man wasn't the only Wu member who experienced life outside of a harsh urban environment for part of his upbringing. For example, Rza spent his formative years living in North Carolina with an uncle named Hollis, who was a doctor.[360] Moving to North Carolina when he was just three years old, Rza would stay there for four years before he returned to Stapleton.[361] This experience outside of Stapleton with a middle class male figure in his life likely opened Rza's eyes to new possibilities beyond the gritty environment he shared with his peers. "That was the man who influenced me," Rza reflected later. "He taught me to have my good nature…all my manners, I learned from him."[362]

Rza also credits his Uncle Hollis with teaching him about science and religion, in addition to exposing him to Southern folk songs whose rhyming couplets bore a startling similarity to the structure and rhythm later associated with rapping.[363] Rza would later go on to incorporate some of the folk rhymes he learned from Hollis in his own rhymes on the Gravediggaz album *Six Feet Deep*, which was released a few months after *ETWT*.[364] Rza was also exposed to positive things during his time in New York City, specifically when he lived in Brooklyn. "I remember being a kid, going to school, [in] P.S. 384, over in Bushwick," Rza recalled. "We would get field trips to the Brooklyn Academy of Music. They would show us films, they'd show us music. Then, we'd go to the Botanical Gardens."[365]

During his formative years as a producer, Rza also spent a significant amount of time far from New York City, when he lived in an apartment in Steubenville, Ohio, with Ghostface and Ol' Dirty Bastard (securing an apartment of his own there after his mother, stepfather and siblings moved to that town).[366] "We started making a lot more demos, just the three of us in Ohio," Rza recalled, in an interview with *XLR8R*. "In 1992, we moved back to New York, got with the rest of our crew that we grew up with, then the Wu-Tang style was born."[367] While it is unclear what influence the change in environment and the small town lifestyle may have had on Rza's production, the change in locale from Stapleton to a more sparsely populated area must surely have given Rza more space to think, if nothing else.[368]

U-God also had some experience traveling outside the New York City area before he joined the Clan, which he noted was something that benefited him when the Clan started touring in earnest. "I traveled before I was with Wu-Tang, to Sacramento, and Jacksonville, so I already knew how to live off the land."[369] The experience that almost half of the Clan had living outside New York City was likely what enabled the Clan to make *ETWT* a broadly accessible record that people across America (and the world) could appreciate.

Of course, everyone who has studied the Clan knows that the housing projects where they spent most of their lives had an indelible impact of their music.[370] Those two housings projects are the Park Hill Apartments and the Stapleton Houses. The Park Hill Apartments are a private, but federally subsidized, apartment community where almost half of the Wu-Tang Clan grew up.[371] The complex is 15 acres and is comprised of multiple six-story buildings.[372] The Park Hill Apartments are located in Clifton, a neighborhood south of Stapleton (the neighborhood where Stapleton Houses is located).[373]

A 2007 media account described the Park Hill Apartments as "one of Staten Island's most notorious, and perhaps most notoriously maligned, communities—a diverse and largely impoverished enclave on the Island's northeast shore."[374] Gerald "Gee-Bee" Barclay, the video director for "Method Man" and "Da Mystery of Chessboxin'," actually directed a documentary about the Park Hill Apartments entitled *Killa Hill.*[375] In addition to being called Killer Hill, at one point the Park Hill Apartments were also called Crack Hill.[376] Adding an international slant beyond the stereotypical image associated with inner city neighborhoods, Clifton and Stapleton house one of the highest concentrations of Liberians outside of Liberia, many of whom fled civil war in Liberia to arrive in a different type of war zone.[377]

Knowing full well the challenges faced by the people who still live in their respective neighborhoods, the Clan often goes back there to inspire others. "Whatever we do, we gonna always come back to the projects. This is our home and they're the new generation coming up. We gotta let 'em know you can get yours in a certain way and stay positive," Raekwon said when discussing the group's affinity for returning to the projects in which they were raised, in an interview filmed on location in the Park Hill Apartments.[378]

The Wu's commitment to staying in close contact with the community where they were raised is just an extension of the family-focused philosophy the group has followed since they started.

"We are a group of men who came together for a common cause," Rza said. "We can't split up—we don't really got too many friends besides us. We may have a thousand people around us, but there's nobody like us. That's the circle right there—that's how come it's so powerful. It ain't brought together for money or women or drugs. We're one in the heart and one in the mind. That's the power of Wu-Tang."[379]

ADDENDUM (11th Chamber)

ETWT was the opening shot in Rza's five-year plan for the Wu's cultural takeover. Method Man's debut *Tical* was the first Wu solo record to launch after *ETWT* and the second salvo fired in the Clan's five-year assault on the *Billboard* charts.[380] Consistent with Rza's strategy to make labels work for the Clan, Loud's marketing of "Method Man," a solo song spotlighting the future star, positioned Meth perfectly for the release of his 1994 solo debut, *Tical*, on Def Jam. To tie in *Tical* to *ETWT*, Rza made the shrewd decision to include a remix of "Method Man" on *Tical*.

Rza also cleverly connected *Tical* to *ETWT* by utilizing the same drum sample that served as the first music heard on *ETWT* as the drum sample for the remix to "Method Man": the iconic drums from Melvin Bliss' "Synthetic Substitution." Furthermore, as aforementioned, this classic drum break was also sampled two other times on *ETWT*, in addition to serving as the sonic foundation for many golden age rap classics, thereby connecting the remix sonically with *ETWT and* a long lineage of classic hip-hop.

The ingenious referencing of pop culture throughout "Method Man" is closely matched by the plethora of cultural references present in the "Method Man" remix. The remix includes new lyrics that add to the universality of the song, most prominently the inclusion of a line from *Schoolhouse Rock*'s "I'm Just A Bill." To assure listener recognition of the reference, Method Man ends the first verse of the remix with the "Bill" line "I hope and pray that I will, but today I am still," just before he starts the chorus (in "I'm Just A Bill," this line is also used just before the chorus).

Meth also adds to the universality of the remix by closing the second verse with a few lines from the classic folk song "Going To Kentucky," half singing several lines from that song ("I'm going to the country/I'm going to the fair/to see the *senorita*/with flowers in her hair"). This line is the second reference containing Spanish in the remix (the first being a line half spoken in Spanish in the first verse: "You ain't got no wins in *mi casa*"), expanding the cultural reach of the song by including a modest bilingual component.[381]

The cultural references in the remix come fast and furious. Paralleling his inclusion of a reference to "pat-a-cake" on the original "Method Man," Meth includes a different nursery rhyme reference on the remix: "a tisket, a tasket." Predating *Tical* by over a hundred years, "A Tisket, A Tasket" originated in America, around 1879.[382] Another reference on the remix reaches back decades to the disco era, specifically the "move it in, move it out" line Method Man delivers in the style of Johnnie Taylor's hook on the 1976 classic "Disco Lady."[383] By referencing disco tunes, nursery rhymes, and folk songs, as well as sprinkling some Spanish words in the remix, Meth created a pop culture gumbo that serves as the perfect illustration of how the Wu reached so many people with their music.

As further proof of the Wu's cultural impact, The Notorious B.I.G. was likely inspired by one line in this remix ("I'm the Buddha Monk on the hunt for machine gun funk") to name one of his songs "Machine Gun Funk" (off of his debut album, *Ready to Die*). Method Man would also appear on that album, at Big's invitation, on a song called "The What." In a possible case of one artist influencing an entirely different commercial medium, McDonald's might have gotten its 1995 ad tagline ("Have you had your break today?") from one Method Man lyric on the remix, "Have you had your Meth today?"[384]

Rza's production, the talent of the Wu's most commercially viable MC and the power of the Def Jam marketing machine combined to assure that Method Man's solo debut, *Tical*, would go platinum. The success of this album had effects that reached far beyond the Clan alone, as *Tical* and (even more so) *Regulate: The G-Funk Era*, the debut album from Warren G, provided Def Jam with the sales they needed in 1994 to recoup from major losses they incurred from investing in commercially unsuccessful groups such as The Flatlinerz and South Central Cartel. It has even been argued, both by Warren G himself and independent observers, that the sales of Warren G's album in particular saved Def Jam from going out of business in 1994, although it is hard to deny that the success of *Tical* (and its platinum Grammy Award-winning single "I'll Be There for You/You're All I Need to Get By") helped Def Jam's fortunes during a rough period.[385]

The next Wu-Tang solo release, 1995's *Return to the 36 Chambers: The Dirty Version* was delivered by Ol' Dirty Bastard, on Elektra Records. This was another smash hit from Wu, also following a period of less than optimal commercial performance from the label that released it. While Elektra had experienced massive success with rock acts like Metallica, its rap roster struggled commercially in 1994, leading up to the arrival of Ol' Dirty Bastard's debut album in March 1995. Elektra rap artists such as Lin Que, Supernatural, and Omniscience all released singles in 1994 that received some critical acclaim, but sold few records. Mainstay Elektra rap act Brand Nubian achieved only modest commercial success with its (Grand Puba-less) second album in 1994 (despite that release coming on the heels of a song placement for the group's "Lick Dem Motherfuckas" on the red-hot *Menace II Society* soundtrack).

Thus, a Wu solo album saved the day again for a label facing a string of commercial misfires, no doubt giving Elektra the confidence it needed to properly back Busta Rhymes' solo debut the following year. Showing the first spark of musical independence in the Clan, Dirty (not Rza) was credited with producing the album's hit lead single, "Brooklyn Zoo," although he later admitted he co-produced that song with True Master.[386]

1995 was the most powerful year for the Wu, in terms of critical reception. The acclaim the Clan received would really ramp up after the release of the two exclusively Rza-produced Wu solo records that followed Dirty's debut. Just five months after the release of *Return to the 36*, Raekwon's *Only Built 4 Cuban Linx* (*OB4CL*) hit the hip-hop world like a hydrogen bomb, debuting as the fourth highest selling album in the country.[387] The album was certified gold just two months later and the all-Rza produced work received rave reviews from critics.

The onslaught continued three months later when Gza dropped his acclaimed second solo album, *Liquid Swords*. In perfect alignment with NGE teachings, *Liquid Swords* was released on the 7th of November (11/7 or Knowledge Knowledge God all being born to Born, in the Supreme Mathematics). The album would go on to be certified gold, for sales of 500,000 copies, within two months of its release. Less than an hour long, *Liquid Swords* was the epitome of Gza's "half short, twice strong" theory of making music more powerful by truncating its length.[388]

During the same year as these iconic releases, the Clan would expand their business empire with the debut of their clothing line, Wu-Wear, which eventually grew to include successful retail outlets on Staten Island and in Atlanta (in addition to other cities). In its first three years of operation, the Staten Island Wu-Wear store would go on to sell $1 million worth of merchandise, a stunning amount for an 800 square foot clothing store focused on a single niche brand (averaging $913 a day, translating to $1.14 per square foot per *day*).[389] Wu-Wear as a whole would sell $10 million worth of merchandise in the same period (meaning that *one* Wu-operated retail outlet accounted for ten percent of the sales for the *entire company*, over the course of three years).[390]

The idea of starting Wu-Wear came from longtime Clan business manager, Oli "Power" Grant. "Through playing around with just fitting the guys for videos and all of that, and always being a kid that was into fashion—the Polo's, the Tommy Hil[figer]'s, and all of that stuff that came before—it just made me want to try to expand out and make another avenue for what we was doing," Power reflected.[391]

Wu-Wear stores expanded to four cities before the chain's expansion finally ended, just before a fifth store could be opened, its first West Coast outlet. "We had New York, Philadelphia, Virginia, Atlanta, and I had one in L.A. but I never fucking opened it…because I kind of knew at that moment I wasn't going to be able to put it together the way I wanted to, so I had to fall back," Power recalled.[392] Power also oversaw licensing for the Wu logo. In exchange for a licensing fee, Power gave permission for the Wu logo to appear on merchandise designed by companies ranging from The Gap (Wu-Tang logo tees) to Nike (1999's Wu-Tang limited edition dunks—likely the first, and possibly the only, rap logo to be featured on a tennis shoe).[393]

The same year as the Nike deal, Sony released the *Wu-Tang: Shaolin* Style video game for PlayStation, the first game where players could assume the role of rappers.[394] Further proving the strength of the Wu brand, Rza's sister, Sophia Diggs, would even go on in 1997 to open a manicure shop called Wu-Nails, across the street from the Staten Island Wu-Wear store.[395]

Rza's personal commitment to the five-year plan was demonstrated by his almost monk-like avoidance of the personal pleasures traditionally enjoyed by rap stars, during the course of that period. "I stayed in the basement for years [making music]," Rza recalled. "I didn't even come outside. I didn't know I was wealthy until 1997. Honestly. I didn't even have sex with no other girls for years—I had one girl, and it was just me and her."[396]

The five-year plan ended with the release of *Wu-Tang Forever* in 1997, coincidentally the year

Rza ended his self-imposed exile. "I broke loose in '97, after I was forsaken," Rza said.[397] Expanding on the theme of being "forsaken" at the request of the interviewer, Rza went deeper. "People you put your trust in, from women to partners, and then they forsake you. Even the Wu-Tang Clan, when Wu-Tang Clan pulled out of the Rage Against The Machine tour, it broke my heart, because I recorded the *Wu-Tang Forever* album with democracy. I let everybody do what they wanted to do. The [older] albums were more like how I wanted it, and it came out better, people say. The [later albums were] more like drama."[398]

As Rza relates above, the Clan reached a major turning point when their tour with Rage Against The Machine fell apart in 1997. Four years after the release of *ETWT*, near the height of Wu's commercial power, iconic political rock group Rage Against The Machine chose Wu-Tang to serve as opening act for their nationwide tour. Many forces conspired against the tour, including police agencies that worked to shut down individual tour dates, sometimes expressing their objection to the content of the lyrics of the two acts.[399]

However, Rza noted that the Wu's participation in the tour was ultimately ended not by outside forces, but by the group's own internal turmoil, as they struggled with their newfound democratic decision-making model. "I told everybody that this was a very important tour for our careers," Rza recounted, reflecting back on the tour, years later. "I said, 'We do this tour right, and first of all, it's going to be trendsetting. We can embed ourselves deeply into American culture. We can go back and do more tours with all the colleges,' [...but the other Clan members didn't see this potential opportunity] because they just wanted to go out and...get it popping. I'm like, 'Fuck that. Let's rock the world. Let's spread our message to the world.' And everybody wasn't understanding that."[400]

One source, online publication *Grantland*, presented an alternative reason for the Clan to back out of the tour: for the opportunity to perform a high profile set at Hot 97's Summerjam, a hugely popular annual concert organized by the most influential urban station in New York.[401] Unfortunately, this huge opportunity did not re-connect the Clan with urban radio. Instead, the performance would result in the Clan being banned from the biggest urban station in the country, after Ghost said "Fuck Hot 97" onstage, in response to the station's decision not to pay to fly the Clan out to perform, a customary perk provided to artists of their stature.[402]

Ghostface's Summerjam rant wasn't the only example of the Clan being forthright when being more diplomatic might have been better from a business perspective. According to rapper/producer Q-Tip, Ol' Dirty Bastard passed on a chance to be on the iconic "Crooklyn Dodgers" single (produced by Tip and Ali Shaheed Muhammad), from the soundtrack to Spike Lee's *Crooklyn*, after noting "ain't nobody getting shot in this movie" when the movie was screened for rappers who were invited to perform on the song.[403] Ol' Dirty Bastard did appear on the soundtrack for *Tales From The Hood*, a much more violent film than *Crooklyn*.[404] Confusingly, however, given his decision not to participate in the *Crooklyn* soundtrack due to the film's non-violent content, Dirty also contributed songs to the soundtracks of films such as *Slam* (1997) and *Bulsworth* (1998), neither of which is considered a violent film.[405]

While ODB's mystifying process of selecting soundtrack appearances might reflect a broader stereotype of the Clan as undisciplined and unpredictable, other Clan members defied easy characterization. "Me and GZA played hundreds of games of chess before we made the songs for *Liquid Swords*," Rza recalled in one interview, describing a cerebral process for crafting a record that would be unusual for any musician, let alone one belonging to a group considered as rowdy as the Wu-Tang Clan.[406]

This is not to say that ODB did not have his serious, thoughtful moments. Although Ol' Dirty Bastard was often viewed as a comical figure, it turns out that one of his more ominous statements should have been taken very seriously. In the middle of his generally light-hearted hit single, "Got Your Money," Dirty exclaimed, "FBI, don't you be watching me."[407] After his death, it was revealed that the FBI had accumulated an astoundingly extensive ninety-four page file on Dirty.[408] None of the matters alleged in the file led to a single prosecution against Dirty, which is shocking because one would presume that extensive surveillance of Dirty would have to be performed to fill up a ninety-four page file, yet none of that surveillance led to the filing of a single criminal charge.

Beyond not leading to any criminal prosecutions, ODB's FBI file perpetuated falsehoods about Dirty as well. A portion of the file repeated the false claim that Dirty engaged in a shootout with NYPD, although the gun Dirty allegedly shot was never found (meaning that the NYPD was apparently shooting at him even though he was unarmed).[409] One witness on the scene stated that what Dirty held in his hand was not a gun, but a cell phone.[410] A Brooklyn grand jury declined to indict Dirty on the specious attempted murder charges brought against him, which were based on NYPD's dubious claim that Dirty shot at police officers (apparently the first instance of a man firing bullets from a cell phone).[411]

This was not the only tragic episode that Dirty survived, nor was it the only time bullets were fired in his direction. On July 1, 1998, Dirty was sleeping when he awoke to find a gun pointed at his face. He wrestled with his assailant, was shot twice, but survived and managed to chase his assailant away.[412]

Dirty being shot at, by police and others, was not the only tragedy the Clan faced during the years following the end of the five year plan, as was particularly exemplified by the imprisonment of Ghostface Killah. In January 1998, just six months after *Wu-Tang Forever* was released, Ghost was sentenced to a three-month prison term after he pled guilty to an attempted robbery in 1995.[413] The case was more complicated than it appeared at first glance, however, as the matter stemmed from Ghost's run-in with parking attendants, after his car's tires were slashed while in their care.[414] When Ghost and his associate saw the tires were slashed, an altercation ensued. Ghost was arrested and faced a 15-year prison sentence unless he pled guilty to the lesser charge of attempted robbery.[415]

This period of incarceration for Ghostface likely harmed the whole group, since Ghost has played an unheralded leadership role in the Wu since the group's inception. Near the time of Ghostface's imprisonment, Raekwon recorded his second solo album, *Immobilarity*, without Ghostface's participation. That album was panned by critics, as were other 1999 efforts from the Clan such as solo debuts from Inspectah Deck and U-God. It wasn't until Ghostface was able to release *Supreme Clientele* in early 2000 that the Clan returned to their former glory, both critically and commercially. The Wu returned to releasing group albums that same year, with *The W* in 2000, quickly followed the next year by *Iron Flag*. The cover to the latter features Ghostface prominently on the left side of the Iwo Jima-inspired cover, the only member not holding the Clan flag (as the rest are doing), perhaps because Ghostface's support of the Clan's artistic mission—their flag—goes unsaid.

As for life in the post-five year plan period for Rza, his presence in pop culture has steadily increased, in both film and music. His directorial debut, *The Man With The Iron Fists*, was co-written by horror film auteur Eli Roth (whose *Hostel* chilled the hearts of many a horror fan) and featured "guest director" Quentin Tarantino, the quintessential pop culture moviemaker who is known for mixing elements from other films to craft his own, similar to how Rza mixes elements from different music genres, when he samples.

In Rza's mind, his work with the Clan and his film work share a clear connection. "All the music I did with the Wu-Tang Clan prepared me to be a director. I didn't know this at the time, of course," Rza explained. "When I got to do the film…having all these great talents under my control was a challenge, but being that I had already dealt with Ol' Dirty Bastard, Method Man, Ghostface, Raekwon, Masta Killa and these guys,

I had a sensibility [about controlling diverse personalities] that became very useful to me."[416] The amount of thought that Rza put into the film is illustrative of his strategic nature. In one interview, Rza explained that "the actual filming took 150 days, but as far as planning [the film, that took] six years."[417]

Rza's artistic output accelerated in 2013, the 20th anniversary of *ETWT*.[418] In September 2013, several media outlets reported that Rza planned to release a 10" vinyl project with arguably the most famous Asian female musician in the world, Yoko Ono (widow of John Lennon of The Beatles).[419] Additionally, Rza executive-produced a new U-God solo record and announced plans to release a collaborative project with Paul Banks, lead singer of critically acclaimed New York indie band Interpol.[420] In 2014, Rza went full circle back to the underground world where Wu thrived over 20 years ago, to collaborate with indie band, Faulkner, who are unsigned as of this writing.[421]

The Wu as a whole continues to resonate through global culture as well, an impact that has been captured in several films. "Method Man" video director Gerald Barclay released *Wu: The Story of the Wu-Tang Clan* in 2008. There is a forthcoming documentary on the life of Ol' Dirty Bastard entitled *Dirty: Platinum Edition*.[422] A film based on the relationship between Dirty and the man who managed him at the time of his death is currently in development, under the working title *Dirty White Boy*.[423] Gza has a long planned documentary on the Wu that has not yet been released, as of this writing.[424]

The Clan also has been featured on several television programs. Method Man had a small role on HBO's acclaimed series, *The Wire*. Dave Chappelle built two skits on his Emmy-nominated series *Chappelle's Show* around Rza and Gza: one skit where they were traded from the Black race to the Asian race in a racial draft and another where they played financial advisors in a fictitious brokerage firm called Wu-Tang Financial.[425]

In a case of either life imitating art or art imitating life, Inspectah Deck admitted in a recent interview that much of his current income derives from investments. "I do other things in life besides rap," Deck said. "There are a couple things that helped keep my lights on when I wasn't rapping. I do mutual funds and all that shit. I got IT investments."[426] Real life Wu-Tang Financial!

It is likely that the next twenty years of the Clan's existence will only solidify their stature in American culture. The impact of the Clan's first twenty years in music is illustrated by the reverence they receive both from iconic acts that predated them and the most commercially successful artists in the current marketplace.

Groundbreaking rap trio De La Soul (whose platinum debut preceded *ETWT* by four years) labeled a 2013 single ("Get Away") as "featuring The Spirit of the Wu," likely because the song heavily sampled both vocals and music from a skit on *Wu-Tang Forever.* In an *XXL* interview, Rza said he was deeply flattered by the gesture. "Posdnuos sent [the song] to me [a] couple of months ago and I cleared it right away," Rza recalled. "I like it. I love De La and…to see De La sampling one of my productions, you know what I mean, that's cool, yo. It gets no cooler than that…."[427]

In a similar vein, platinum-selling rap star Drake entitled the second promotional single from his 2013 album, *Nothing Was The Same*, "Wu-Tang Forever," utilizing the resulting social media frenzy around the track's title for his own gain, by offering the track for immediate download to any fan who pre-ordered his album.[428] Few rappers ever receive such homage from a popular contemporary, let alone twenty years after their debut album was released.

When asked how he felt about the semi-tribute, Rza explained that not only did he support Drake's "Wu-Tang Forever" song, he actually made its commercial release possible, through his clearance of that record's vocal sample ("It's yours") and incorporation of several lines from Raekwon's opening verse (both taken from "It's Yourz," off of the *Wu-Tang Forever* album).[429] "[Drake] sent me [the] song because they couldn't clear the sample. So I did it myself, personally, for free. Free of charge," Rza revealed. "Because, to me, that's what we meant when we said Wu-Tang is forever. We didn't think we were going to live forever. We meant that the energy of what we do would spread on in culture, generation by generation. And by Drake absorbing it and having that influence in his life and having it be a part of him, it proves what I'm saying. And I'm really proud that he chose that rap."[430]

Drake is not alone amongst popular contemporary rappers in his reverence for the Wu. Another top-selling act of 2013, Macklemore, referenced the Clan very favorably in his recent multi-platinum single "Can't Hold Us," by noting in the beginning of that song's second verse that he was "raised by Wu-Tang." Reviewing *ETWT* near its 20th anniversary for the magazine *XXL*, Macklemore continued his effusive praise for the Clan, by explaining the pivotal role that album had in his childhood and by commenting on the group's iconic status. "I remember starting to listen to it when I was in the sixth grade, so I was probably a little bit late from when it first dropped, but once I found it, it became the soundtrack to my entire existence," Macklemore wrote. "They've solidified their place as the greatest Hip Hop group of all time."[431]

Fans of hip-hop entered the Wu-Tang's 36 chambers over twenty years ago. It's doubtful that we will leave any time soon.

Critical Acclaim for *Enter the Wu-Tang: 36 Chambers*[432]

- *101 Albums That Changed Popular Music* (2009) [No Order][433]
- *1001 Albums You Must Hear Before You Die* (2005) [No Order][434]
- *Blender—500 CDs You Must Own Before You Die* (2003) [No Order]
- *Blender—The 100 Greatest American Albums of All Time* (2002) #59
- *CDNOW—The 10 (+5) Essential Records of the 90s* (2002) [No Order]
- *Consequence of Sound—Top 100 Albums Ever* (2010) #62[435]
- *Dance de Lux* (Spain)—*The 25 Best Hip-Hop Records* (2001) #5
- *DJ Magazine* (UK)—*The Top 50 Most Influential Dance Albums Since 1991* (2006) #38
- *Ego Trip—Hip Hop's 25 Greatest Albums by Year 1980-98* (1999) #1
- *Entertainment Weekly—The 100 Best Albums from 1983 to 2008* (2008) #42[436]
- *FNAC* (France)—*The 1000 Best Albums of All Time* (2008) #90
- GQ (UK)—*The 100 Coolest Albums in the World Right Now!* (2005) #35
- *Guardian* (UK)—*1000 Albums to Hear Before You Die* (2007) [No Order]
- *Helsingin Sanomat* (Finland)—*50th Anniversary of Rock* (2004) [No Order]

- *Hervé Bourhis* (France)—*555 Records* (2007) [No Order]
- *Juice* (Australia)—*The 100 (+34) Greatest Albums of the 90s* (1999) #40
- *Les Inrockuptibles* (France)—*50 Years of Rock 'n' Roll* (2004) [No Order]
- *Les Inrockuptibles* (France)—*The 100 Best Albums 1986-1996* (1996) #59
- *Mojo* (UK)—*Mojo 1000, the Ultimate CD Buyers Guide* (2001) [No Order]
- *Mojo* (UK)—*The 100 Greatest Albums of Our Lifetime 1993-2006* (2006) #62
- *MUZIQ* (France)—*200 Records for a Dream Collection* (2007) [No Order]
- *New Musical Express* (UK)—*Top 100 Albums of All Time* (2003) #82
- *Nude as the News*—*The 100 Most Compelling Albums of the 90s* (1999) #61
- Paul Morley (UK)—*100 Greatest Albums of All Time* (2003) [No Order][437]
- *Pitchfork*—*Top 100 Favorite Records of the 1990s* (2003) #36
- *Q* (UK)—*90 Albums of the 90s* (1999) [No Order]
- *Record Collector* (UK)—*10 Classic Albums from 21 Genres for the 21st Century* (2000) [No Order]
- *Rock & Folk* (France)—*The Best Albums from 1963-1999* (1999) [No Order]
- *Rock de Lux* (Spain)—*The 150 Best Albums from the 90s* (2000) #25
- *Rock de Lux* (Spain)—*The 200 Best Albums of All Time* (2002) #178

- *Rolling Stone—The 100 Greatest Albums of the 90s* (2010) #29
- *Rolling Stone—The 500 Greatest Albums of All Time* (2003) #386
- *Rolling Stone—The Essential Recordings of the 90s* (1999) [No Order]
- *Rolling Stone* (Germany)—*The 500 Best Albums of All Time* (2004) #453
- *Select* (UK)—*The 100 Best Albums of the 90s* (1996) #21
- *The Source—The 100 Best Rap Albums of All Time* (1998) [No Order]
- *Sounds* (Germany)—*The 50 Best Albums of the 1990s* (2009) #33
- *Spex* (Germany)—*Albums of the Year* (1993) #23
- *Spin—The 125 Best Albums of the Past 25 Years* (2010) #32
- *Spin—Top 100 (+5) Albums of the Last 20 Years* (2005) #20
- *Spin—Top 90 Albums of the 90s* (1999) #22
- *Technikart* (France)—*50 Albums from the Last 10 Years* (1997) [No Order]
- *The Sun* (Canada)—*The Best Albums from 1971 to 2000* (2001) [No Order]
- Tom Moon—*1000 Recordings to Hear Before You Die* (2008) Main Entry
- *Treble—Top 100 Albums of the 90s* (10 per Year) (2008) #6
- *Various Writers—Albums: 50 Years of Great Recordings* (2005) [No Order]
- *Vibe—100 Essential Albums of the 20th Century* (1999) [No Order]

- *Vibe—150 Albums That Define the Vibe Era* (1992-2007) [No Order]
- *Vibe—51 Albums Representing a Generation, a Sound and a Movement* (2004) [No Order]
- *Visions* (Germany)—*The Most Important Albums of the 90s* (1999) #67
- *VOLUME* (France)—*200 Records That Changed the World* (2008) [No Order]

Ratings[438]

All Music Guide—**5 Stars**

Le Guide du CD (1995-1997)—**4 Stars**

MusicHound (1998-99)—**5 Bones**

Robert Christgau, *Consumer Guide*—**A-**

Rolling Stone—**5 Stars**

Piero Scaruffi—**7**

The Source—**4.5 mics**[439]

Spin's Book of Alternative Albums (1995)—**8**

Martin C. Strong, *The Great Rock Discography*—**8**

Virgin Encyclopedia of Popular Music (2002)—**4 Stars**

Wu-Tang Clan
Selected Discography[440]

Group albums appear underlined, solo albums appear with asterisk*

1991
Words From The Genius (Gza)* (Cold Chillin'/ Warner Bros.)

1993
Enter the Wu-Tang: 36 Chambers (Loud/Sony) (platinum)[441]

1994
Six Feet Deep (Gee Street) (Gravediggaz [Rza, Prince Paul, Frukwan and Poetic]) (gold)
Tical (Method Man)* (Def Jam) (platinum)

1995
Return to the 36 Chambers: The Dirty Version (Ol' Dirty Bastard)* (Elektra) (gold)
Only Built 4 Cuban Linx (Raekwon featuring Ghostface Killah)* (Loud/Sony) (gold)
Liquid Swords (Gza)* (Geffen) (gold)

1996
Ironman (Ghostface Killah featuring Raekwon and Cappadonna)* (Razor Sharp/Sony) (platinum)

1997
Wu-Tang Forever (Loud/Sony) (4x platinum)

The Pick, The Sickle and The Shovel (Gee Street) (Gravediggaz [Rza, Prince Paul, Frukwan and Poetic])

1998

Tical 2000 (Method Man)* (Def Jam) (platinum)
Bobby Digital in Stereo (Rza)* (Gee Street) (gold)

1999

Beneath The Surface (Gza)* (Geffen)
*N***a Please* (Ol' Dirty Bastard)* (Elektra) (gold)
Uncontrolled Substance (Inspectah Deck)* (Loud)
Immobilarity (Raekwon)* (Loud) (gold)
Golden Arms Redemption (U-God)* (Wu-Tang Records/Priority)

2000

Supreme Clientele (Ghostface Killah)* (Razor Sharp) (gold)
The W (Loud/Sony) (platinum)

2001

Iron Flag (Loud/Sony) (gold)
Bulletproof Wallets (Ghostface Killah)* (Epic)

2002

Legend of the Liquid Sword (Gza)* (Geffen)

2003

The Lex Diamond Story (Raekwon)* (Ice H20/ EMI)

2004

No Said Date (Masta Killa)* (Nature Sounds)

Tical 0: The Prequel (Method Man)* (Def Jam) (gold)

The Pretty Toney Album (Ghostface)* (Def Jam)

2005

Grandmasters (Gza/DJ Muggs) (Angeles Records)

2006

Made In Brooklyn (Masta Killa)* (Nature Sounds)

Fishscale (Ghostface Killah)* (Def Jam)

2007

The Big Doe Rehab (Ghostface Killah)* (Def Jam)

<u>8 Diagrams</u> (SRC/Universal)[442]

2008

Pro Tools (Gza)* (Babygrande)

2009

Ghostdini: The Wizard of Poetry in Emerald City (Ghostface Killah)* (Def Jam)

Only Built For Cuban Linx Pt. II (Raekwon)* (Ice H2O/EMI)

2010

Wu-Massacre (Ghostface Killah, Raekwon and Method Man) (Def Jam)

2011

Shaolin vs. Wu-Tang (Raekwon)* (Ice H20/EMI)

2012

Wu-Block (Ghostface Killah/Sheek Louch) (E1)
Selling My Soul (Masta Killa)* (Nature Sounds)

2013

Twelve Reasons To Die (Ghostface Killah)* (Soul Temple Records)
Keynote Speaker (U-God)* (Soul Temple Records)

Wu-Tang Clan
Selected Filmography[443]

1993
Wu-Tang Nation (documentary)

1997
One Eight Seven (Method Man)
Cop Land (Method Man)

1998
Belly (Method Man)*

1999
Ghost Dog: The Way of the Samurai (Rza)* (acting and scoring)
Black and White (Raekwon, Meth, Deck, Ghost and Wu business manager Power)

2001
How High (Method Man)*

2003
Coffee and Cigarettes (Rza and Gza)*

2004
Garden State (Method Man)
Soul Plane (Method Man)
U-God: Rise of a Fallen Soldier (documentary)

2007
American Gangster (Rza)

2008

Wu: The Story of the Wu-Tang Clan (documentary)

2010

Due Date (Rza)*

2011

The Sitter (Method Man)

2012

*The Man With The Iron Fist** (Rza, as star/co-writer/director/music composer)
Red Tails (Method Man)

2013

G.I. Joe: Retaliation (Rza)

2014

Brick Mansions (Rza)
The Protector 2 (Rza)[444]
The Cobbler (Method Man)[445]

[1] *See* http://nymag.com/anniversary/40th/50665/. Herc would later be credited with creating the sound of hip-hop by spinning two records back to back to extend the breakbeat—the instrumental breakdown in records—at his Bronx parties. *See* http://youtu.be/_BcJRnoGJeM?t=5m34s

[2] *Enta Da Stage* did not have an immediate commercial impact, but over the course of 13 years, it eventually sold 350,000 copies in the U.S. *See* http://www.sputnikmusic.com/review/7671/Black-Moon-Enta-Da-Stage/. This is roughly a third of the sales that *ETWT* would attain in two years, as it was certified platinum on May 15, 1995, meaning one million copies of the album were shipped to retailers. *See* http://riaa.com/goldandplatinumdata.php?content_selector=gold-platinum -searchable-database.

[3] As mentioned in the prior endnote, "platinum" signifies that one million copies have been shipped to retailers to be sold to the public. "Multi-platinum" signifies that several million albums have shipped to retailers to be sold.

[4] On Jive, for one 1993 example, West Coast artists Too Short (*Get In Where You Fit In*) and Spice 1 (*187 He Wrote*) were certified platinum and gold (500,000 records sold), respectively, despite tepid critical response, while a more critically acclaimed release that year, from East Coast artist

KRS-ONE (*Return of the Boom Bap*), did not see the same level of sales. There are exceptions, of course. Def Jam's South Central Cartel sold poorly, in contrast to their East Coast labelmates, for example.

[5] See *The Big Payback*, by Dan Charnas, p. 348 (New American Library, 2010).

[6] Nas would not sell nearly what the Clan or The Notorious BIG sold, but he would markedly outsell critically acclaimed East Coast albums that preceded *ETWT*, such as the album where Nas first appeared on wax, Main Source's *Breakin' Atoms*. Nas was also a close associate of the Wu and was one of the first names thanked in the liner notes of *ETWT*, under his original stage name: Nasty Nas. For another example of the Clan's familial bond with Nas, he and Mobb Deep were the only non-Clan rappers ODB mentioned when he listed which emcees he was down with, in a 1995 interview. *See* http://youtu.be/V0YWQk7l0hg

[7] *See* http://blogs.villagevoice.com/music/2011/03/ten_reasons_why.php

[8] See *In the Name of Elijah Muhammad: Louis Farrakhan and The Nation of Islam*, by Mattias Gardell, p. 224 (Duke University Press Books, 1996).

[9] The idea that the 120 Lessons are a distilled version of the teachings of the Nation of Islam is

described most concisely in the introduction to *Knowledge of Self: A Collection of Wisdom on The Science of Everything in Life*, edited by Dr. Supreme Understanding Allah, CBS Allah and Sunez Allah, p. 8-9 (Supreme Design Publishing 2009) ["…the foundation of the lessons—the Supreme Mathematics made such a complex subject as the universe and its workings, impressively simple to understand. This innovation and insight into the science of everything in life produced a methodology ready for application by anyone in any age group. This process also elevates the insightful teachings of the Nation of Islam, extracted and distilled as our 120 Lessons, into a mathematical system of study and development."].

See also *The Five Percenters: Islam, Hip-Hop and the Gods of New York*, by Michael Muhammad Knight, p. 52 (Oneworld Publications 2008) [discussing Allah teaching up to 40 youth at a time]. See also *The Wu-Tang Manual*, by Rza and Chris Norris, p. 44 (Riverhead Trade, 2005). ["The father felt that endangered poor black youth required a faster approach to the teachings than the one the Nation was offering and so he broke the lessons down to their core, what followers call 'the 120'—120 lessons or 'degrees'."].

[10] *See* http://www.realitysandwich.com/devil_deep_space_birth_azrael_wisdom. The choice of intersection likely was not coincidental, as the number 7 signifies God in The Supreme

Mathematics. The school still stands at 2122 Adam Clayton Jr. Boulevard, a stretch of 7th Avenue, north of Central Park, re-named in memory of the late iconic black congressman. *See* http://universalbuilders.ning.com/profiles/blogs /gods-and-earths-in-your-area-1. The school's exact location is closer to 7th & 126th, but it is popularly associated with the intersection of 7th & 125th.

[11] See *Encyclopedia of Muslim-American History*, edited by Edward E. Curtis, p. 115 (Infobase Publishing, 2010).

[12] While Rza states "In Divine Mathematics, the Z stands for Zig-Zag-Zig" on page 4 of the *Wu-Tang Manual*, he breaks down the Z in his name differently on the very next page in the book. "R-Z-A. It stands for Ruler-Knowledge-Wisdom-and-Understanding Allah." See *The Wu-Tang Manual*, pp. 4-5. On "Wu-Tang: 7th Chamber," off of *ETWT*, Rza refers to himself as Ruler Zig-Zag-Zig Allah.

[13] Rza revealed in *The Wu-Tang Manual* that Gza's name was initially spelled Jizza, a shortened version of Justice, the second half of Gza's divine name in NGE, Allah Justice. See *The Wu-Tang Manual*, p. 8.

[14] While he will readily admit that the Nation of Gods and Earths influenced him, Ghostface has gone on record to say that he was never a

member of the Nation of Gods and Earths. *See* http://allhiphop.com/2004/06/02/ghostface-change-gon%C2%92-come/ ["I'm not a part of the Five Percent Nation. I always respected what the brothers spoke about, but I was never a part of it."]

[15] See *The Wu-Tang Manual*, p. 63. In a 1993 interview with pioneering video show *Yo! MTV Raps*, the group was asked "Who is responsible for putting [Wu-Tang Clan] together?" Method Man responded "Gza, Rza and Ghost." *See* http://youtu.be/bMdCcA egJQ4?t=1m46s

[16] *See* http://vimeo.com/30103392 (this film is also sometimes titled *Shaolin Vs. Wu-Tang*).

[17] See *Wu-Tang Manual*, p. 74. "After The Laughter Comes Tears" was an independently released version of the track "Tearz" that subsequently appeared on the group's debut album, *ETWT*.

[18] In a recent video interview, Masta Killa recounted how he decided not to go to the recording session where "Protect Ya Neck" was created, due to his decision to avoid being truant from a night school G.E.D./B.A. program in which he was enrolled. *See* http://youtu.be/TEDj C6Q9Z9w

[19] "b/w" is an abbreviation for "backed with" and is a shorthand description denoting that a record has two sides, with the A-side listed first, followed by b/w, while the B-side is listed last.

The single was split into the Shaolin Side ("After The Laughter") and the Wu-Tang Side ("Protect Ya Neck"), instead of the usual A-side and B-side. Close inspection of the single reveals, however, that the "Protect Ya Neck" side was labeled "PR234A" and the "After The Laughter" side was marked "PR234B," raising the inference that "Protect" was considered the A-side and "After" was considered the B-side. "Protect" was also the only side with a radio edit and A-sides are traditionally the sides marketed to radio. *See* http://cfile24.uf.tistory.com/image/27553A4650ED8C8820B051

[20] See *The Big Payback*, p. 439-440.

[21] See *The Tao of Wu*, by Rza, p. 107 (Riverhead Trade, 2010) ["While there were other labels that wanted to sign us—some offering as much as $200,000—most of them wanted to sign the whole group, including any solo efforts. But I knew a sum like that wouldn't be enough money to support us…[s]o instead we signed with Rifkind for a fraction of the money, but with the freedom to solicit ourselves to other labels and make solo deals."].

[22] Rza's discussion of that iconic session can be found on page 75 of *The Wu-Tang Manual*.

[23] U-God corresponded with the author via Twitter, where he made this claim on January 13, 2014. *See* https://flic.kr/p/nrjnAS

[24] *See* http://www.complex.com/music/2011/10/method-man-25-essential-songs/wu-tang-clan-protect-ya-neck-1993

[25] *See* http://www.redbullmusicacademy.com/magazine/yoram-vazan-interview. To add another variation on the story, future Wu business manager Oli "Power" Grant recalled paying for the majority of the studio costs related to recording "Protect Ya Neck" himself. *See* http://passionweiss.com/2011/02/28/question-in-the-form-of-an-answer-oli-power-grant-of-wu-tang-clan/

[26] See *The Wu-Tang and Rza: A Trip Through Hip-Hop's 36 Chambers*, by Alvin Blanco (Praeger 2011), p. 13. Sources published nearer to the release date of *ETWT* tend to stick to the 10,000 sales figure. See *Rappages*, February 1994, p. 46, "Wu-Tang Clan: 36 Chambers of Death...Choose One" by Cheo Coker. I have been unable to find any writers who have reported the 10,000 unit sales figure who cited a source for that number.

[27] In a book published almost twenty years after the single was released, Rza claimed the single sold *over* ten thousand copies. See *The Tao of Wu*, p. 107. Perhaps over the course of almost twenty years, Rza had forgotten the exact number of sales for "Protect Ya Neck" and gave an estimated number. It should also be kept in mind that it was Divine, not Rza, who was responsible for tracking sales of the single, so Rza may not

even know the exact number of units the single sold independently. See *The Big Payback*, p. 438. Published in 2009, *Hip-Hop In America: A Regional Guide* also claims "Protect Ya Neck" sold "over 10,000 copies," although this source appears to include sales that "Protect Ya Neck" attained after Loud re-released the single, in addition to its independent sales, as it refers to the single as "Protect Ya Neck" b/w "Method Man," i.e. the version of the single that Loud distributed. See *Hip-Hop In America: A Regional Guide*, edited by Mickey Hess (Greenwood 2009), p. 130.

[28] See *The Big Payback*, p. 438. It is possible that there was an additional pressing of the single, after the initial 10,000 units were all either given to DJs or sold, but I can find no source indicating this occurred before the Loud re-release (or at any time after the re-release). Rza noted the single was put out in October 1992 and the deal with Loud was on the table by March 1993. See *The Tao of Wu*, p. 106-107.

[29] See *The Big Payback*, p. 439. "12 inches" is frequently used as a synonym for vinyl singles. The name derives from the fact that vinyl singles in the modern era are usually 12 inches in diameter, as contrasted with the diameter (7 inches) associated with earlier singles. *See* http://en.wikipedia.org/wiki/Gramophone_record

[30] Getting assistance with mailing out the single also made things easier for the four men

(including Rza) who ran Wu-Tang Productions, all of whom had their hands full with various responsibilities. Mook and Power worked on getting the single in stores; Divine kept track of billing, sales and collection of monies owed from sales of the single. See *The Big Payback*, p. 438. Those three men still play a key role in Wu-Tang's business management today.

Proving again that Wu is a family affair, Divine is Rza's brother. *See* http://www.hiphopdx.com/index/news/id.6214/title.u-god-sues-wu-tang-music-group-for-170-000 Mook is Rza's cousin. See *The Tao of Wu*, p. 106.

[31] See *The Big Payback*, p. 438.

[32] See *The Tao of Wu*, p. 107.

[33] The Loud-distributed version of the single, according to Rza, sold 30,000 copies between March, when they signed with Loud, and April 1993. See *The Tao of the Wu*, p. 107.

[34] See *Billboard*, November 15, 1997 issue, p. L4. This information was printed in a sidebar, in an advertising supplement, likely paid for by Loud itself. The claim is presumptively valid, since it is dubious that Billboard would print an ad with such a claim about its own charts if the claim were erroneous. The advertising supplement appeared in the middle of a retrospective article on Loud Records.

[35] I have had some difficulty identifying exactly which radio personalities were featured in those interludes. *See* http://rapgenius.com/Wu-tang-clan-wu-tang-clan-aint-nuthing-ta-fuck-wit-lyrics #note-498596 [the citation for "Jason Staton" on that page alleges that this Michigan State University radio personality was the one interviewing Method Man and Raekwon during the *ETWT* interlude in question, using as its source a January 18, 2007 comment left at http://konstantkontakt.blogspot.com/2007/01/stretch-armstrong-bobbito-kcr-111892.html at 1:13 PM].

Will Strickland communicated with the author via email and wrote that Staton was someone who helped with promoting Wu-Tang in the Midwest, but could not confirm that Staton was the radio host interviewing the Clan on *ETWT*. He could, however, recall a different college radio DJ playing a role in the album. According to Strickland's recollection, Martin Moore & DJ Riz's WNYU show was the sampled show on the *ETWT* interlude where a caller requested to hear Wu-Tang. When reached via Twitter by the author, twenty years after *ETWT*'s release, DJ Riz seemed not entirely sure when asked if his show was the source of the call-in segment sampled on the album, replying "I think so." *See* https://flic.kr/p/nrjbND

[36] One prominent example of Tribe's Afrocentrism is their decision to name the

opening song on *Midnight Marauders* after iconic South African rebel Steve Biko. Although listed as Track 2, this is the first actual song on the record, beginning right after the spoken intro. Both Tribe and Wu were influenced by Islam, particularly Tribe member Ali Shaheed Muhammad. Years after the release of *ETWT*, Tribe frontman/ producer Q-Tip also converted to Islam. *See* http://www.spin.com/articles/spin-interview-q-tip/

[37] *See* http://www.hiphopdx.com/index/news/id.26195/title.q-tip-says-ol-dirty-bastard-rza-battled-him-in-high-school

[38] See *The Big Payback*, p. 444

[39] *See* http://wutangclan.com/2013/11/15/wu-forever-celebrating-20-years-of-wu-tang-part-1-2-and-3/ [from the beginning of Part 3]. An independent researcher, Dan Charnas, confirmed that "Method Man" was one of the first rap singles played heavily once Hot 97 switched its format from dance to hip-hop. See *The Big Payback*, p. 348.

[40] *See* http://web.archive.org/web/20140303092958/http://www.wired.com/entertainment/music/magazine/15-11/pl_music (audio from bonus interview at the bottom of the page). Sadly, as of June 2014, the original link to the *Wired* interview now appears to be dead, so I had to utilize the archive.org version for citation purposes. The

author of the article is Steven Leckart and it was published on 10/23/2007 in *Wired* Issue 15.11.

A Tribe Called Quest's highest selling record had only gone gold before their third album, *Midnight Marauders* (released on the same day as *ETWT*) went platinum. Since Tribe had no platinum records at the time *ETWT* was recorded, Rza's statement—including Tribe amongst acclaimed acts that had not yet gone platinum in 1993—was historically accurate.

[41] Both elements are foundational to the lives of the Clan, as both NGE philosophy and martial arts film were introduced to the Clan in their childhood and informed their development into men. The impact of NGE on the Clan is discussed more thoroughly in Chapter 7.

[42] Coincidentally, the influence of Asian culture on the Clan may have been related to NGE teachings, wherein Black Americans were referred to as Asiatic, not African, which also overlaps with NOI teachings that the Black race derived from Asia. See *Transnational Blackness*, edited by Manning Marable and Vanessa Agard-Jones, p. 251 (Palgrave Macmillan, 2008) (quoting a speech Malcolm X gave in New York where he purportedly said "Who is the Original Man? The Honorable Elijah Muhammad has taught us the truth. It is the Asiatic Black Man. Why do we say the Asiatic Black Man? Why not the African Black Man…?" followed by the answer: "Originally this

entire planet (that is now called Earth) was called Asia. The first man on it was the Black Man.") [citing as its source a July 11, 1957 FBI teletype transcript].

Rza's initial exposure to NGE, from Gza, occurred close in time to his early experiences watching martial arts films depicting elements of Asian (specifically Chinese) culture, likely magnifying his interest in Southeast Asia. Clarence 13X was also a martial arts instructor during his time in the Nation of Islam. *See* http://en.wikipedia.org/wiki/Clarence _13X. It would not be far-fetched to argue that the Father's interest in martial arts might possibly have influenced his adherents to also develop an affinity for the martial arts as well.

[43] See *The Wu-Tang Manual*, p. 60.

[44] *See* http://www.filmcomment.com/article/rzas -edge-the-rzas-guide-to-kung-fu-films

[45] See *Check The Technique: Liner Notes for Hip-Hop Junkies*, by Brian Coleman, p. 450 (Villard Books, 2005).

[46] Although usually described as a Brooklyn resident, Gza included "Killah Hills 10304," a vivid crime story rap seemingly named after Park Hill, on *Liquid Swords*. *See* http://www.barrypopik .com/index.php/new_york_city/entry/killa_hill_ or_killer_hill_park_hill_staten_island. The title of the song aside, "Killah Hills 10304" is more of a

generic crime story rap (with tales of evading customs and hits in Manhattan steakhouses) than a song specifically about Park Hill. *See* http://rapgenius.com/Gza-hells-wind-staff-killah-hills-10304-lyrics. One 2012 *New York Times* article stated that Gza grew up in Park Hill, without citing a source. *See* http://www.nytimes.com/2012/11/18/nyregion/columbia-professor-and-gza-aim-to-help-teach-science-through-hip-hop.html?_r=0 [published November 16, 2012 in the print version]. This *Times* article is the only source I have uncovered describing Gza as a Park Hill resident. In a documentary where U-God listed Park Hill residents in the Wu, he omitted Gza, later referring to Gza as a Brooklyn resident, in the same documentary. *See* http://youtu.be/1Z48HnRCXa0?t=2m 50s.

[47] See *Encyclopedia of Muslim American History*, p. 596. *See also* http://wu-international.com/WuTangClan/AllInTogether Now.html

[48] *See* http://www.xlr8r.com/features/2008/09/rza -beyond-shaolin

[49] *See* http://www.youtube.com/watch?v=a0TqJtaFRhc (accessed July 18, 2013)

[50] ODB co-produced "Da Mystery Of Chessboxin" with Rza, although the general public seems unaware of this contribution. ODB is an acronym for the late Ol' Dirty Bastard.

---

[51] *See* http://www.youtube.com/watch?v=a0TqJ taFRhc

[52] *See id.*

[53] *See* http://exclaim.ca/Features/Timeline/wu-tang_clan-days_of_wu. Sadly, Rza's mother died in 2000, just seven years after the release of *ETWT*. *See* http://hiphopwired.com/2014/05/11/exclusive-rza-reflects-last-converasation-with-his-mother/?utm_source=twitterfeed&utm_med ium=twitter

[54] See *The Tao of Wu*, p. 25.

[55] *See* http://halftimeonline.net/portfolio/inspect ah-deck-wu-tang/ (accessed June 22, 2013)

[56] *See* http://www.rollingstone.com/music/news/wu-tang-family-values-19970710#ixzz2pJHF7g O3

[57] Red Bull Music Academy interview, RBMA Music Academy 2011. *See* http://vimeo.com/301 03392 [at 17:20 mark]

[58] *See* http://www.youtube.com/watch?v=A6S4 fMX6FWA (accessed June 25, 2013)

[59] See *Check The Technique*, p. 452.

[60] At least one source, a Canadian online publication, claims that "Meth Versus Chef," a track on which Method Man and Raekwon exchanged a series of combative short verses, was

birthed in this tradition, when the two men battled for the chance to rhyme over a Rza beat. "Meth Versus Chef" appeared on Method Man's solo debut *Tical*, released a year after *ETWT*. *See* http://exclaim.ca/Features/Timeline/wu-tang_clan-days_of_wu/Page/2

[61] See *Check The Technique*, p. 460.

[62] *See* http://www.filmcomment.com/article/rzas-edge-the-rzas-guide-to-kung-fu-films (accessed September 21, 2013).

[63] See *Check The Technique*, p. 452 ["At the time [when the single was out] I got arrested and had bail for like ten thousand dollars, and I figured the record company could throw up ten G's to get me out…[but] they gave me my contract back. I was going to put Wu-Tang out on Tommy Boy, but I realized I had to just do my own shit," said Rza]. The legal troubles Rza faced in Steubenville are discussed in greater detail in Chapter 9.

[64] Street teaming (or street promotion) is a practice wherein a group of people pass out free music to potential customers and put up stickers and posters on public space, often without permission, to maximize promotional visibility for artists about to release records. Street promotion was done by others before Rifkind, such as Doug Young, Lionel Ridenhour and Jeff House (working with West Coast indie Macola), but once those three men teamed up with Rifkind, he was

the first to convince major labels to pay for the street promotions service, starting with Capitol Records. See *The Big Payback*, p. 444.

[65] *See* http://news.radio.com/2013/04/11/radio-com-essentials-enter-the-wu-tang-clans-coachella-chamber/

[66] *See* http://content.time.com/time/arts/article/0,8599,88545,00.html#ixzz2fU7dmP8z (accessed September 20, 2013). One source claims that every Wu solo deal had a clause that reserved 20% of all revenue generated by the deal for Wu-Tang Productions and that the solo deals were all joint ventures with Wu-Tang Productions. *See* http://exclaim.ca/Features/Timeline/wu-tang_clan-days_of_wu/Page/2. This might have only been the case, however, for the early solo deals, as by 1996 (for example), Ghostface's deal was a joint venture between Razor Sharp Records and Sony.

[67] By one account, the advance for the Loud deal was "only" $60,000. *See* http://www.npr.org/blogs/therecord/2013/04/08/176519640/the-wu-tang-clans-20-year-plan. While this could still be considered a large amount of money for a group from upbringings as austere as the Clan, split nine ways this sum was not very substantial, even by the standards of recording advances of that era.

[68] *See* http://vimeo.com/30103392 [Red Bull Music Academy interview 2011, roughly at 7:30 mark].

[69] *See* http://www.spin.com/#articles/wu-tang-clan-enter-the-wu-tang-36-chambers-oral-history/

[70] *See* http://vimeo.com/30103392 [Red Bull Music Academy interview, 2011, roughly at 7:40 mark].

[71] See *The Wu-Tang Manual*, p. 74.

[72] *See* Red Bull Music Academy interview, 2011.

[73] *See* http://www.redbullmusicacademy.com/magazine/yoram-vazan-interview

[74] *See* http://www.spin.com/#articles/wu-tang-clan-enter-the-wu-tang-36-chambers-oral-history/ When Vazan said the Clan made Firehouse their home, he might have been more literal than one would expect. The Brooklyn studio had been converted from a thousand square foot two-bedroom loft, but judging from the description of the condition the Clan kept the studio, as described by album cover photographer Daniel Hastings, the Clan had virtually converted it back to a loft. "I [came] back to New York and went to talk with the RZA in the studio when they were finishing the album," Hastings reflected. "The studio was called Firehouse. And it was the most disgusting studio I've ever seen in my entire career. This place had holes in the walls, wires were coming out of the walls, chicken wings all on the floor, blunt wraps all over the place, empty 40s all over. The place was insane, dude." *See* http://www.egotripland.com/making-of-wu-tang

-clan-36-chambers-album-cover-photographer-daniel-hastings/

[75] *See* http://www.redbullmusicacademy.com/magazine/yoram-vazan-interview.

Vazan recalls the total cost of the "Protect Ya Neck" session being "around $300 or so."

[76] See *Rappages*, February 1994, p. 45, "Wu-Tang Clan: 36 Chambers of Death...Choose One" by Cheo Coker. Rakeem is the divine name for Rza, the name by which fellow NGE adherents might likely refer to him, and part of his original stage name (Prince Rakeem). Rakeem was also likely the name that Ryman most often heard Rza called by fellow Clan members during the recording of *ETWT*.

[77] *See* http://www.spin.com/#articles/wu-tang-clan-enter-the-wu-tang-36-chambers-oral-history/

[78] See *Wu: The Story of The Wu-Tang Clan* [http://www.youtube.com/watch?feature=player_detailpage&v=YkoZY_-XG_c#t=1631]

[79] *See Billboard*, April 2, 1994, p. 22, "The Rap Column," by Havelock Nelson ("Wu-Tang Clan's Loud/RCA album *Enter The Wu-Tang (36 Chambers)* was certified gold by the RIAA").

[80] *See* http://riaa.com/goldandplatinumdata.php?content_selector=gold-platinum-searchable-database. *See also* http://en.wikipedia.org/wiki/RIAA

_certification (for definition of the terms "gold" and "platinum").

[81] "Phantoms of the Hip Hopera" by RJ Smith, *Spin*, July 1997, p. 70, 72. Both Stetsasonic and De La Soul were signed to Tommy Boy when Rza was signed there as Prince Rakeem. Though the exact timing of this conversation is not described by Paul, it is possible that the conversation took place somewhere near the time when Prince Paul assisted Rza in producing his debut single, "Ooh, I Love You Rakeem," well before the Wu had any prospect of being signed as a group, let alone spawning multiple solo record deals. *See* http://www.xlr8r.com/features/2008/09/rza-beyond-shaolin ["Produced with the help of Prince Paul, ['Ooh We Love You Rakeem'] channeled the tongue-in-cheek vibe of Biz Markie…"].

[82] *See* http://www.youtube.com/watch?feature=player_detailpage&v=YkoZY_-XG_c#t=816. Ironically, Rifkind would later go on to sign not just the Clan, but the group Malone mentioned signing to Island himself: Mobb Deep. To add further irony to Bonz Malone not understanding the Eastern influence on Wu-Tang's music, "bonze" means "Buddhist monk" and the Shaolin monks who inspired the Clan were Buddhists. *See* http://www.thefreedictionary.com/bonze. *See also* http://www.honggia.net/index_e.htm [discussing how the teachings of various bonzes were central to one particular Shaolin temple]. The name Bonz is actually a play on Fonz (from the TV show

Happy Days) and a creative spelling of the word "bones." See http://blackadelicpop.blogspot.com/011/03/bonz-malone-interview-2007.html Although Bonz's name is not derived from the word "bonze" at all, the visual similarity between Bonz and "bonze" is ironic, nonetheless.

[83] *See* http://youtu.be/BWml7yoFwHA?t=59s (accessed June 25, 2013).

[84] *See* http://www.npr.org/blogs/therecord/2013/04/08/176519640/the-wu-tang-clans-20-year-plan

[85] See *Wu: The Story of The Wu-Tang Clan* (documentary DVD)

[86] See *Wu: The Story of The Wu-Tang Clan* (documentary DVD)

[87] Rza would also go on to sample a line ("You want to fight? Fight with me. One to one, man to man") from this film later, for the song "Meth vs. Chef," which appeared on Method Man's debut album.

[88] The opening credit sequence to the film *Mystery of Chessboxing* features men fighting on a chessboard, which parallels the visual imagery of warriors fighting on a chessboard in the music video for "Da Mystery of Chessboxin'." Ghostface Killer, the villain (antihero?) in the film, appears at the very beginning of the film and engages in the non-villainous act of allowing what

appears to be the wife and child of a victim he kills to escape, while he fights (and eventually kills) the target of his scorn. Additionally, Ghostface Killer (the film character) fights with a style known as the five elements. Ironically, hip-hop is comprised of five elements as well (emceeing, deejaying, breaking, graffiti writing and the lesser-known fifth element: knowledge). *See* http://www.zulunation.com/hip_hop_history_2.htm

[89] *Shaolin & Wu-Tang*, like many films sampled by Rza, was produced by the Shaw Brothers film studio.

Sir Run Run Shaw, who ran the Shaw Brothers film studio with his brother Ronnie Shaw, passed away on January 7, 2014. *See* http://www.npr.org/blogs/thetwo-way/2014/01/07/260446322/run-run-shaw-kung-fu-movie-pioneer-dies

[90] In the "Protect Ya Neck" video, Ghostface's name is spelled "Ghost Face Killer." His name is also spelled Ghost Face Killer in the *ETWT* liner notes. Subsequently, Ghost Face was made one word (Ghostface) and the spelling of "Killer" was changed to "Killah."

[91] See *The Wu-Tang Manual*, p. 20. IMDB.com, the official database for the biographies of a diverse range of film and TV professionals, lists the spelling of the actor's name as Siu Tin Yuen, although—to Rza's credit—the spelling of his

name appears to vary from film to film. The same actor has, in different films, been billed as Yuan Siu Tin, Simon Yuen, Yuen Hsiao-Tien, and Hsao Ten Juan. The character that Rza refers to as The Chef has been billed by various names, such as Master Cook [*Ninja Checkmate*] or Cook/Teacher [*Jade Claw*], although perhaps there is some U.S. version where he was billed as The Chef. *See* http://www.imdb.com/name/nm0803298/?ref_=fn_al_nm_1

[92] *See* http://en.wikipedia.org/wiki/Shaolin_ and_ Wu_Tang (this film is also occasionally titled *Shaolin Versus Wu-Tang*). *Shaolin & Wu-Tang* is also the source of the vocal sample that dramatically closes the album—"It's our secret! Never teach the Wu-Tang!"

[93] *See* http://www.imdb.com/title/tt0080002/?ref_=fn_al_tt_1 [which lists the U.S. release date as September 1981].

[94] *See* http://www.thefreedictionary.com/en+garde

[95] *See* http://www.urbandictionary.com/define.php?term=sharp (Definition #4). Sharpness has also long been used as a descriptor for sound in hip-hop, as the sound of a DJ manipulating a turntable is referred to as "cutting" as often as it is referred to as "scratching."

---

[96] *See* http://www.youtube.com/watch?v=c_1xsQBgRTM

[97] *See* http://youtu.be/bMdCcAegJQ4?t=46s

[98] The concept of music as a form of combat—with a range of discordant sounds battling for the listener's attention—is exemplified on that song. "On 'Bring Da Ruckus' you'll hear a garbage can mixed with finger snaps and a piano in a whole different key," Rza said, when discussing how he put together the track. "Then you have the distorted bass which is really the only thing that is in sync. You have all this going on then I sampled a CD skipping and used that for my horns! D-D-D-D-D-D-D! I didn't have a horn so I did that. People went, 'He makes music outta noise!'" *See* http://www.dazeddigital.com/music/article/16679/1/dazed93-rzas-ghetto-symphonies

[99] The Palestine Liberation Organization (PLO) has since evolved into an internationally recognized political party.

[100] "Macs" are slang shorthand for two particularly lethal types of sub-machine gun: the Mac-10 and the Mac-11. There is admittedly an off-hand chance that Raekwon intended his line "Rolling like 40 Macs" to refer to "40 macks" (as in, pimps), but that doesn't really fit the aggressive content of the rest of his verse.

[101] This film is the source of *ETWT*'s *36 Chambers* subtitle. The album is often called simply "36 Chambers" by fans of the Clan.

[102] See *China Forever: The Shaw Brothers and Diasporic Cinema*, edited by Poshek Fu, p. 236 (University of Illinois Press 2008). One could even argue that there is a parallel between the Clan and *The Thirty Sixth Chamber*'s plot about government oppression. In hip-hop, corporations attempted to destroy the culture (the village), then the Clan came to avenge the culture's destruction and return a fresh new style to the people. Admittedly, although the Clan was successful in acquiring a unique recording deal for themselves, they were unfortunately unable to do much to change how corporations interact with (or interfere with) hip-hop culture. Still, they certainly brought a new style (a 36th chamber!) to the masses with *ETWT*!

[103] Rza described the Tiger Style as "[a] hard external style that meets force with force…[with] kicking maneuvers [that] are usually low…" and Crane Style as "[a] system in which the fighter keeps his arms wide, makes winglike movements, [and] uses high kicking…." See *The Wu-Tang Manual*, p. 65. Visualizing these styles as described by Rza, one can imagine how complicated a fight between two combatants using those respective styles could become, thus outlining the heart of Ol' Dirty Bastard's boast about his style being like a "Tiger versus Crane" fight. It's a colorful way of saying his style is unorthodox, like a bout between

fighters using those two oddly matched fighting styles.

Another vocal sample from a vintage martial arts film that references a specific fighting style can be found on the track immediately following "Chessboxin'." In fact, "Wu-Tang Clan Ain't Nuthin' To F' Wit" begins with a sample of the phrase "Tiger style," a combat style featured prominently in the 1977 Shaw Bros. movie *Executioners From Shaolin* (the film from which the "tiger style" intro is sampled). *See* http://sard less.com/wu-tang-moviesamples.html. *See also* http://en.wikipedia.org/wiki/Executioners_From _Shaolin.

[104] *See* http://sardless.com/wu-tang-movie-samples.html

[105] *See* http://web.archive.org/web/20140303092 958/http://www.wired.com/entertainment/musi c/magazine/15-11/pl_music [from the full audio interview at the bottom of the page]

[106] *See* http://youtu.be/YkoZY_-XG_c?t=22m 41s

[107] One look at footage from a 1993 Wu performance at the Uptown Comedy Club should clearly demonstrate Method Man's appeal, as women in the crowd begin screaming as soon as he starts his "Protect Ya Neck" verse. *See* http:// youtu.be/vw-GQBN J3nA?t=1m3s

[108] See *Vibe*, March 1995, p. 81.

[109] It should be noted that utilizing pop references in hardcore rap had been popularized previously by Das Efx on their hit single "They Want Efx," which was released in March 1992, well before the release of "Method Man" in 1993. *See* http://en.wikipedia.org/wiki/They_Want_EFX.

Raekwon's recent admission that Wu-Tang was patterned after Hit Squad in a 2011 Red Bull Music Academy presentation is particularly important to note here, since Das Efx was part of the Hit Squad (although, of course, there is no vocal similarity at all between Meth and Das Efx). *See* http://vimeo.com/30103392 (near the 11:00 mark). However, in an interview with the Combat Jack show, Raekwon notes that Method Man paralleled Redman (not Das Efx), particularly from a visual perspective. *See also* http://the combatjackshow.com/uncategorized/video-rae kwon-talks-why-he-and-ghostface-are-the-epmd-of-the-wu-tang-clan/#.UZw1vuvpJdA

Finally, it should also be noted that some Wu lyrics were written years before they were recorded, so it is entirely possible that Method Man wrote "Method Man" several years before it was recorded in March of 1993. *See* http://en.wiki pedia.org/wiki/Method_Man_(song)

[110] *See* http://en.wikipedia.org/wiki/Method_Man _%28song%29 (listing the single's release date).

[111] *See* http://www.youtube.com/watch?v=pq3YdpB6N9M (accessed May 16, 2013).

[112] *See* http://en.wikipedia.org/wiki/Pat-a-cake,_pat-a-cake,_baker's_man (accessed May 16, 2013). See also *Oral and Literate Culture in England, 1500-1700*, by Adam Fox, p. 202 (Oxford University Press, 2002) [quoting dialogue from Fardell saying "...And pat a cake, pat a cake, bakers [sic] man..." in *The Campaigners*]. *See also* http://www.rhymes.org.uk/pat_a_cake_pat_a_cake.htm

[113] *See* http://en.wikipedia.org/wiki/Green_Eggs_and_Ham (accessed May 16, 2013)

[114] See *The Supreme Understanding: The Teachings of Islam in North America*, by Abdul Noor, p. 171 (iUniverse Inc., 2002) [asking rhetorically "How can one become a 5%er?" then responding with a series of lifestyle choices, including "…abstain from poisonous animals (pork)…"]. Azarel, an early follower of Father Allah, recounted a story of Father Allah telling a god to go away for 30 days for eating ham. See *The Five Percenters*, p. 245.

[115] *See* http://web.archive.org/web/20051225125934/http://www.publishersweekly.com/article/CA186995.html

[116] *See* http://en.wikipedia.org/wiki/I_Tawt_I_Taw_a_Puddy_Tat_(song). The ad lib that follows the Tweety line ("yippie yay yippie ya yippie yo") appears to be a homage to George Clinton's 1982 hit "Atomic Dog" (the

background vocal in the hook of which goes "bow wow wow, yippie yo, yippie yay, bow wow yippie yo, yippie yay"), a possible homage made all the more likely by the line that follows it, wherein Method Man warns the pussycat he saw that it should "beware" of the "diggy dog shit right here." Layering metaphors, Meth is likely using "pussycat" as code for calling his imaginary opponent a "pussy," i.e. a weak male figure, who can't compete with Meth's more aggressive "dog" persona.

[117] Dr. Bill Cosby outlined the cultural and educational value of Fat Albert in his 1976 dissertation "An Integration of the Visual Media via 'Fat Albert and the Cosby Kids.'" *See* http://scholarworks.umass.edu/dissertations/AAI7706369/

[118] *See* http://youtu.be/QfzDUpB88x4

[119] *See* http://youtu.be/9UmNluMt2s4? at the 4:53 mark (accessed May 16, 2013). "Super Sporm" [sic] was most famously referenced by Boogie Down Productions on "Superhoe," off of their *Criminal Minded* debut album.

[120] *See* http://youtu.be/OAd43DwAbn0 (accessed May 16, 2013).

[121] *See* http://www.whosampled.com/sampled/Tootsie%20Pops/. As testimony to the enduring cultural resonance of the "How Many Licks" ad campaign, Tootsie Roll Industries reported on its

website that it has been receiving mail from children since 1970 attempting to guess how many licks it takes to get to the center of a Tootsie Roll Pop. *See* http://www.tootsie.com/comp_faq.php

[122] *See* http://www.youtube.com/watch?v=BWml7yoFwHA (accessed June 25, 2013).

[123] *See* http://online.wsj.com/article/SB10001424052702303640104577436392955009490.html (accessed June 15, 2013). Many would concede that Method Man, the only other Wu member with a solo cut on *ETWT*, was considered the group's most marketable member, hence the Clan's decision to spotlight "Method Man" rather than "After The Laughter" on the Loud-distributed re-issue of the group's debut single.

[124] Ghostface is also the first member to rhyme on the album, following Rza's "Bring Da Ruckus" hook. Rza emphasizes this fact in *The Wu-Tang Manual*, implying that he deliberately sequenced the album in a way that assured that Ghostface was the first MC heard on *ETWT*, to highlight his importance to the group. See *The Wu-Tang Manual*, p. 22. To hammer the point home, that specific Ghostface verse starts with Ghostface saying his own name.

[125] *See* http://en.wikipedia.org/wiki/The_Shaolin_Drunken_Monk

[126] The drunken monk motif goes beyond just the aforementioned *The Shaolin Drunken Monk* and can be found in martial arts cinema standouts such as 1978's *Drunken Master*. In *Drunken Master*, the eponymous protagonist utilized a "drunken" fighting style. This is the film that originally popularized the "drunken fist" fighting style and may possibly have been the film Gza was referencing in his "drunken monk" reference on "Clan In Da Front." *See* http://en.wikipedia.org/wiki/Drunken_Master

[127] Also, an example of NGE tradition appears in the intro to "Can It Be All So Simple," when Rza responds to an interrupting voice with "I'm building, I'm building." "Building" is an NGE tradition of analyzing anything deeply utilizing the Supreme Mathematics, breaking down the meaning of words with The Supreme Alphabet or just assigning new meaning to words by deciphering their components, such as breaking down the word "history" to "his story"—in reference to the Eurocentric, patriarchal slant through which the past is recounted in many Western history books. NGE teachings are discussed more in depth in Chapter 7, including a breakdown of the song "Wu-Tang: 7th Chamber," a track which heavily references the NGE worldview. For that reason, "Wu-Tang: 7th Chamber" is the only song on the tracklisting that I will not discuss in this chapter.

[128] This particular roll call ends with ODB making what may be the most epic introduction of all time, for Ghostface. Just to show he can't be predicted, Rza inserts Method Man's hook after the introduction, when the average listener would expect Ghost to begin rhyming immediately after ODB's introduction.

[129] The roll call for Clan members is also reminiscent of comic books Rza read as a youth, where writers were careful to explain who characters in a superhero group were in captions on the intro page, sometimes even including a brief outline of a superhero group's origin—as well as individual group member's names—in the opening page of every issue.

[130] "Psyche" is a slang term, pronounced and sometimes spelled "sike" (rhyming with "strike"), indicating that the speaker just played a trick on the listener (akin to saying "April Fools!"). In this line, psyche/sike is used to mean that Ghost has tricked the listener by saying "speaking of the devil" when he's actually speaking of himself, a god, according to NGE teachings.

[131] Even Inspectah Deck's name is indicative of the Clan's love of pop culture, as the "Inspector" part of Inspectah Deck's stage name was inspired by Inspector Clouseau, from *The Pink Panther*. See *The Wu-Tang Manual*, p. 28.

[132] *See* http://stuffpoint.com/kung-fu-movies/image/181441/fatal-flying-guillotine-dvd-cover-picture/

[133] Coincidentally, in the Supreme Mathematics, two signifies wisdom and five signifies power. The idea of the Clan trading wisdom for power (two for five) is apt when, with *ETWT*, they provided their listeners with street wisdom in their lyrics in exchange for power in the music industry, power built on their rabid fanbase's support.

[134] See *Icons of Hip Hop: An Encyclopedia of the Movement, Music, and Culture*, Vol. 2, edited by Mickey Hess, p. 367 (Greenwood Icons, 2007).

[135] *ETWT* engineer Carlos Bess posted on an online studio gear forum that he played live drums on "Wu-Tang: 7th Chamber Part II." *See* http://www.gearslutz.com/board/3926467-post23.html

Later releases of the album featured the "Method Man" remix as the closing track. The "Method Man" remix is discussed extensively in the addendum. It also should be noted that the vinyl version of the album has a different tracklisting than the CD or cassette version. *See* http://en.wikipedia.org/wiki/Enter_the_Wu-Tang_(36_Chambers). The CD/cassette tracklisting is the order of the songs that will be referenced throughout this book.

136 *See* http://www.spin.com/#articles/wu-tang-clan-enter-the-wu-tang-36-chambers-oral-history/

137 *See id.*

138 *See* http://www.egotripland.com/making-of-wu-tang-clan-36-chambers-album-cover-photo grapher-daniel-hastings/2/. Sometimes the fog of memory leads to conflicting accounts between eyewitnesses. As testament to that, the number of members listed in this Hastings quote seemingly contradicts Murphy's account that two of the masked figures on the cover were not Clan members, since seven figures are visible on the cover and the editorial changes to Hastings' quote (in brackets) indicate that six Clan members were present. The simplest way to resolve the discrepancy appears to be to blame the publication (*egotripland.com*) for adding Raekwon to the quote (in brackets) even though Hastings is only on the record as listing five members as being present.

This theory would also presume that Hastings somehow forgot to mention that Raekwon was one of those who were absent when he listed the missing members. It's also possible that shots including the two additional non-Clan hooded figures were never used in the final cover image selected. Corroborating part of Hastings' story, there is video of Wu-Tang Clan performing in hoodies and masks, purportedly at the Jack The

Rapper convention event in question. *See* http://www.themeaningofdope.com/?p=158

[139] Hastings also made a point to note that initially Rza wanted to wait for the entire group to be present, but unnamed Loud executives shot down the idea of doing another shoot as cost prohibitive ["So RZA was like, 'Yo, man, we need the whole crew here.' I was like, 'This is it. We got to do something because we're not spending any more money on these guys.' I didn't know if the Wu-Tang Clan was gonna sell records or not. The executives were like, 'We already spent a few thousand dollars on this. Get something.'"]. *See* http://www.egotripland.com/making-of-wu-tang-clan-36-chambers-album-cover-photographer-daniel-hastings/2/

[140] "Piano stab" is a hip-hop production term for random sharp piano notes sampled and interspersed throughout a composition. As such, a listener should not be surprised to find piano "stabs" incorporated into the individual sampled pieces that form the music in "Bring Da Ruckus," a track that is the audio equivalent of a swordfight.

[141] As such, *ETWT* was a clarion call for a return to the original values of hip-hop, in an era when West Coast gangsta rappers, dance rap from MC Hammer and Vanilla Ice, and gimmick rappers like Another Bad Creation seemed to be on the verge of spinning the genre far from its New York foundation.

In the end, of course, even the most criticized of these commercial successes wound up widening the appeal of hip-hop, as new listeners were drawn into the culture by the millions. One hip-hop writer, Junichi Semtisu, has admitted that MC Hammer's "Can't Touch This" was his introduction to the art of sampling, writing in a 2005 piece that he had no idea that hip-hop songs were constructed from sampled sounds before that song was released. *See* http://www.o-dub.com/weblog/2005/03/loving -sample.html

[142] Although it is unclear whether those choices were deliberate, utilizing the same drums on the opening track and the two solo tracks on the album might subconsciously lead the listener to always connect their initial experience with the album with those two solo performances. As a result, the listener would still associate the Clan as a whole with both solo efforts and those two tracks wouldn't "stand apart" from the group effort. In light of all the evidence demonstrating the forethought Rza put into every move the Clan made in their early years, an argument that Rza might engage in this type of subtle cross-branding is not completely unreasonable.

There is one more interesting thing to note about this sample choice, namely its title. "Synthetic substitution" is a mathematical concept and mathematics is vital to the Clan, due to their allegiance to NGE. Admittedly, there is little evidence that Rza's devotion to mathematics influenced his selection of this funky breakbeat, merely for its title. His re-use of it three times on one album lends some credence to this theory, though.

[143] Amazingly, Johnson, born in 1936, outlived ODB and is still alive as of this writing. *See* http://en.wikipedia.org/wiki/Syl_Johnson.

Mississippi-born when Jim Crow was at its most powerful, Johnson was a conscious artist and his thoughtful soul classic "Is It Because I'm Black" was later sampled by Rza for the Wu-Tang Clan song "Hollow Bones."

[144] A line ("took away our native tongue") at the 0:33 mark of a different New Birth song, "African Cry," inspired the name of a hip-hop supercrew that preceded Wu-Tang Clan: Native Tongues. The story of how the Native Tongues collective got their name is discussed in depth in the Tribe Called Quest documentary, *Beats, Rhymes and Life*. *See* http://www.imdb.com/title/tt1613023/

As mentioned earlier, *ETWT* was released on the same day as popular Native Tongues affiliate group A Tribe Called Quest's third album, *Midnight Marauders*.

[145] Pitch shifting vocal samples from soul records would later become the most noticeable aspect of Kanye West's early production work and he has openly given Rza credit for inspiring him. This technique was used in classic rock records by

Chuck Berry and, later, by The Beatles. *See* http://en.wikipedia.org/wiki/Pitch_shift.

Rza went on to co-produce the opening song on Kanye's *My Beautiful Dark Twisted Fantasy* album. Unfortunately, this contribution later led to a copyright infringement suit. *See* http://www.holly woodreporter.com/thr-esq/rza-protecting-his-neck-sampling-425107.

146 *See* http://en.wikipedia.org/wiki/The_Way_ We_Were_(song). The Streisand original won both an Oscar and a Golden Globe for Best Original Song.

147 *See* http://en.wikipedia.org/wiki/Labi_ Siffre

148 *See* http://www.whosampled.com/sample /4435/Wu-Tang-Clan-Wu-Tang-Clan-Ain't-Nuthing-Ta-Fuck-Wit-Lafayette-Afro-Rock-Band-Hihache/

149 Interview with the author, via Twitter. *See* https://flic.kr/p/nHNQHv. Method Man stated in this exchange that he suggested the use of the drum sample on that record, without naming the sample (per hip-hop tradition). A different source claims the drum break used on "Wu-Tang Clan Ain't Nuthin' To F' Wit" was "Hihache". *See* http://www.whosampled.com/sample/4435/Wu -Tang-Clan-Wu-Tang-Clan-Ain't-Nuthing-Ta-Fuck-Wit-Lafayette-Afro-Rock-Band-Hihache/. *See also* See https://www.youtube.com/watch ?v=Aa9LVMNsLXw

[150] *See* http://www.factmag.com/2014/02/04/sample-the-funk-10-legendary-samples-and-the-stories-behind-them/4/

[151] When Method Man mentioned suggesting the "Nuthin' To F' Wit" drum sample when he was contacted by the author, via Twitter, he also used the hashtag "shout to Biz Markie," apparently to attribute Biz Markie as an artist who used that iconic breakbeat before the Clan—on Biz's 1987 song, "Nobody Beats The Biz." *See* http://www.whosampled.com/sample/9757/Biz-Markie-T.J-Swan-Nobody-Beats-the-Biz-Lafayette-Afro-Rock-Band-Hihache/. This recognition of artists who came before them is key to the Clan's commitment to keeping hip-hop traditions alive.

[152] Interestingly, "Method of Modern Love" was remixed by Arthur Baker, one of hip-hop's earliest producers, best known for his work on hip-hop classic "Planet Rock" (1982), by Afrika Bambaattaa and the Soulsonic Force. "Planet Rock" was the 12-inch that led Tommy Boy Records to invest heavily in releasing hip-hop records. Several years later, Tommy Boy would sign Rza to his first solo deal as Prince Rakeem. See *The Big Payback*, by Dan Charnas, pp. 78-80 [discussing how "Planet Rock" was the third single released by Tommy Boy and its first major success—certified gold on September 16, 1982].

[153] Although Rene missed her chance at stardom while on Stax, she was phenomenally lucky in one

respect: she narrowly avoided a lethal plane crash. Rene backed out at the last minute from an opportunity to join Stax labelmates Otis Redding and several members of The Bar-Kays on an ill-fated December 1967 plane trip that ended tragically in a crash, killing almost everyone on board. Only one of the plane's occupants, a member of The Bar Kays, survived. *See* http://www.gomemphis.com/news/2012/feb/16/cover-story-unsung-stax-star-gets-due/?print=1

[154] The line would have so much resonance that multi-platinum rapper 50 Cent would re-use it over ten years later, utilizing the same cadence as Meth, on his song "Funeral Music". *See* https://www.youtube.com/watch?feature=player_detailpage&v=6Rt5ORTVNbg#t=106

[155] *See* http://en.wikipedia.org/wiki/Fame_%28Irene_Cara_song%29. The song also won a Golden Globe award for Best Original Song in 1980 as well. *See id.*

[156] *See* http://www.dazeddigital.com/music/article/16679/1/dazed93-rzas-ghetto-symphonies

[157] *See* http://www.filmcomment.com/article/rzas-edge-the-rzas-guide-to-kung-fu-films

[158] See *China Forever: The Shaw Brothers and Diasporic Cinema*, p. 229.

[159] *See id.*

[160] *See id.* at 231.

[161] The *Shaolin & Wutang* line of dialogue "If what you say is true, the Shaolin and the Wu-Tang could be dangerous" sets off the beginning of *ETWT*, leading into the opening track "Bring Da Ruckus." As the Wu-Tang master dies, his last words to his surviving student are "It's our secret! Never teach the Wu-Tang!," a vocal sample Rza chooses to close the Clan's iconic debut album.

[162] The term "jewel" is applied by NGE adherents to any valuable piece of knowledge or advice. The term is likely connected to the NGE philosophy regarding The Twelve Jewels (twelve things everyone needs to live in civilization, including: knowledge, wisdom, understanding, freedom, justice, equality, food, clothing, shelter, love, peace and happiness). See *Five Percenter Rap: God Hop's Music, Message, and Black Muslim Mission*, by Felicia Miyakawa, p. 36 (Indiana University Press, 2005).

[163] *See* http://web.archive.org/web/20140303092958/http://www.wired.com/entertainment/music/magazine/15-11/pl_music

[164] *See* http://www.thedailyshow.com/watch/thu-march-24-2005/rza

[165] *See* http://web.archive.org/web/20140303092958/http://www.wired.com/entertainment/music/magazine/15-11/pl_music (the full audio interview is at the bottom of the page)

---

[166] *See* http://www.youtube.com/watch?v=c _1xs QBg RTM&

[167] *See* http://en.wikipedia.org/wiki/Method_Man _%28film%29. The film was re-titled *Method Man* when it was released on video in America. *See* http://www.imdb.com/title/tt0079142/releaseinf o?mode=desktop

[168] *See* http://www.imdb.com/title/tt0081097/. In one interview shot years after *ETWT* came out, Dirty revealed that Rza gave him his stage name. *See* https://www.youtube.com/watch?v= V0YWQk7l0hg&feature=player_detailpage#t=46

Poppa Wu, a father figure for the entire Clan, says that ODB was called Dirty since he was a child, due to his early problems with hygiene. *See* http://www.youtube.com/watch?feature=player_ detailpage&v=tjcjkRx6wHM#t=144.

Yet another source claims that the idea for Dirty's stage name came about because Dirty worked at a garage where he often got quite dirty. *See* http://exclaim.ca/Features/Timeline/wu-tang _clan-days_of_ wu.

[169] *See* http://en.wikipedia.org/wiki/Tiger_and_ Crane_Fist. Admittedly, there are several martial arts films that utilize Tiger clans and Crane clans in combat sequences. Dirty referenced the Tiger and Crane clans again in the subtitle to "Brooklyn Zoo II (Tiger Crane)" off his debut album, *Return to the 36th Chamber: The Dirty Version.*

[170] This style of weaving titles into an extended metaphor was later perfected by Gza on "Labels," off his debut album, *Liquid Swords*.

[171] *See* http://vimeo.com/30103392 [Red Bull Music Academy interview, 2011, at 20:00 mark].

[172] *See* http://www.youtube.com/watch?v=11aXvISC9bA (at roughly the 0:30 mark).

[173] *See* http://www.thedailyshow.com/watch/thu-march-24-2005/rza (near the 1:30 mark) (accessed September 20, 2013)

[174] *See* https://listenrecovery.wordpress.com/category/danny-hastings-photos/. Hastings emigrated to New York City in pursuit of a career in photography. Before shooting the cover to *ETWT*, Hastings shot the cover to KRS-ONE's *Return of the Boom Bap* (released two months before *ETWT*). After photographing the cover of *ETWT*, Hastings went on to shoot album covers for such hip-hop classics as Gangstarr's *Moment of Truth* and Raekwon's *Only Built For Cuban Linx*, not to mention shooting Blackstar's classic debut video, "Definition." *See id.*

[175] *See* http://www.discogs.com/artist/Carlos+Bess#t=Credits_Instruments-Performance&q=&p=1 [establishing Bess' ethnicity]. *ETWT*'s liner notes specifically read: "Engineered by Ethan Ryman, except 'Da Mystery of Chessboxin' engineered by Carlos Bess."

In a twist connecting the Clan to the world of visual art, Ryman's father was Robert Ryman, a pioneering figure in several art movements, including monochrome painting and minimalism. *See* http://en.wikipedia.org/wiki/Robert_Ryman.

Years after *ETWT* was recorded, Ethan Ryman went on to become a visual artist himself. *See* https://www.facebook.com/pages/Ethan-Ryman-Studio524-Project-Space/319766031370162?sk=info

The 20th Anniversary of *ETWT* led several artists to connect the Wu to the art world in a more tangible way, by organizing an art exhibit commemorating the anniversary at a gallery named Wallplay, in New York City. *See* http://blog.pantone.com/2014/01/triumph-20-years-of-the-wu-tang-clan/

[176] *See* http://www.redbullmusicacademy.com/magazine/yoram-vazan-interview

[177] *See id.*

[178] *See* http://www.spin.com/#articles/wu-tang-clan-enter-the-wu-tang-36-chambers-oral-history/

[179] *See* http://www.spin.com/#articles/wu-tang-clan-enter-the-wu-tang-36-chambers-oral-history/. Ryman recalling that "Shame" was the first song he engineered with Wu gives credence to Vazan's recollection that Bess (not Ryman) engineered pre-*ETWT* recordings "Protect Ya

Neck" and "After The Laughter Comes Tears," unless "Shame" was recorded before both of them.

180 *See* http://www.redbullmusicacademy.com/magazine/yoram-vazan-interview

181 *See* http://sterling-sound.com/engineers/chris-gehringer/#biography

182 *See* http://www.spin.com/#articles/wu-tang-clan-enter-the-wu-tang-36-chambers-oral-history/

183 *See* http://www.spin.com/#articles/wu-tang-clan-enter-the-wu-tang-36-chambers-oral-history/

184 *See* http://web.archive.org/web/20140303092958/http://www.wired.com/entertainment/music/magazine/15-11/pl_music (the audio version of the interview is at the bottom of the page)

185 *See* http://web.archive.org/web/20140303092958/http://www.wired.com/entertainment/music/magazine/15-11/pl_music. Rza appears to have been referring to *The 36th Chamber of Shaolin* here.

186 *See* http://network.yardbarker.com/nfl/article_external/detroit_lions_kicker_learned_english_from_wu_tang_clan/14252489?linksrc=home_rg_head_14252489

187 *See* http://www.kpopstarz.com/articles/40902/20130909/gdragon-wu-tang-clan-big-bang.htm

[188] *See* the Filmography section of this book to see a list of key film titles where Method Man was featured. Admittedly, Meth had two small parts in *Copland* and *187*, respectively, the year before *Belly* was released, but *Belly* was arguably his breakout role.

[189] Only the video for "C.R.E.A.M." (directed by Ralph McDaniels) comes close in terms of visual quality. *See* http://www.vibe.com/article/20-years-36-chambers-uncle-ralph-talks-directing-wu-tangs-early-videos. Finally, Hype Williams' split video for "Wu-Tang Clan Ain't Nuthin To F' Wit" backed with "Shame On A Nigga" is mainly comprised of shots from other Wu videos interspliced with performance footage, so few would argue that it is the best-directed *ETWT* video. Nonetheless, it is noteworthy for the strobelight effect present during Rza and Method Man's verses, which may have influenced the lighting effects utilized in the subsequent Gza-directed split video, "Shadowboxing" backed with "4th Chamber," both songs off of his *Liquid Swords* album.

[190] The drive-by shooting was widely considered the assassination method of choice for West Coast gang members at the time. A direct link to the Eiht cameo is here: http://youtu.be/7m148vZDwJA?t=2m16s

[191] In 1989, New York rap trio 3rd Bass dissed popular Oakland artist MC Hammer at the end of

their video "The Gas Face" and on the last verse of "The Cactus." *See* http://youtu.be/QYp28t EAVvs?t=4m1s. *See also* http://rapgenius.com/3rd-bass-the-cactus-lyrics.

In 1990, KRS-ONE espoused possibly the earliest statement of coastal pride in rap by telling listeners "Now I'm gonna show you how the East Coast rocks" on the Boogie Down Productions song, "Original Lyrics." *See* http://youtu.be/xTlG xqcjgwE?t=2m33s. In 1992, Brooklyn duo Das Efx sampled this KRS line on a song called "East Coast" that is mostly stream-of-consciousness, but contained a dis to West Coast artist Gerardo, known mostly for his song "Rico Sauvé."

In 1991, Bronx rapper Tim Dog released "Fuck Compton" in response to the rise of gangsta rap artists from that city, including MC Eiht's group, Compton's Most Wanted. *See* http://en.wikipedia.org/wiki/Fuck_Compton

Twenty-one years after *ETWT* was released, the Wu would ironically inspire up-and-coming Compton rapper YG Hootie to name a single "36 Chamber Flow." *See* http://youtu.be/DcA6jnjsr Dw.

[192] *See* http://www.complex.com/music/2013/03/the-50-greatest-fashion-moments-in-rap-video-history/raekwon-can-it-all-be-so-simple (accessed May 17, 2013)

[193] *See* http://www.birthplacemag.com/2008/12/capturing-the-clan-wu-tang-documentary-director-gerald-barclay/

[194] See *Wu: The Story of the Wu-Tang Clan* DVD. There were rumors near this period that Ghostface was always masked in the early videos because he was on the run from the law, but it is difficult to locate an independent source to verify this claim.

[195] Kurt Anthony's name can be seen for a fraction of a second under the title "Protect Ya Neck," as the video starts. *See* http://youtu.be/R0IUR4gkPIE. Anthony is also credited with directing "Protect Ya Neck" in the "about the author" section of the Amazon page for his 2012 novel, *Street Queens* and in the Wikipedia page on Method Man's videography. *See* http://www.amazon.com/Street-Queens-Kurt-Anthony-ebook/dp/B009F0LF9Q. *See also* http://en.wikipedia.org/wiki/Method_Man_videography

[196] *See* http://www.hiphopdx.com/index/editorials/id.2220/title.-enter-the-wu-tang-20-years-later-an-oral-history

[197] *See* http://youtu.be/YkoZY_-XG_c?t=20m17s

[198] *See* http://www.vibe.com/article/20-years-36-chambers-uncle-ralph-talks-directing-wu-tangs-early-videos.

[199] *See The Wu-Tang Manual*, p. 8.

[200] While a hat with the Hiero logo will cost you $25, a baseball cap with the Wu logo on it costs $37. *See* http://shop.wutangclan.com/collections/hats. *See also* http://store.hieroglyphics.com/index.php?route=product/category&path=65_80.

A sampling of random Wu fans wearing Clan paraphernalia can be found at these two sites: http://wudisciples.blogspot.com/2014/02/wu-mamis-tuesday-89.html and http://www.xxlmag.com/news/2014/02/children-wu-tang/.

See also http://www.sfweekly.com/2000-03-01/music/having-it-both-ways/ [establishing that Del designed the Hieroglyphics logo]. See also *Hip Hop Matters: Politics, Pop Culture, and the Struggle for the Soul of a Movement*, p 116, by S. Craig Watkins (Beacon Press 2005) [establishing that Chuck D created the Public Enemy logo]

[201] *See* http://www.hiphopdx.com/index/news/id.15583/title.ghostface-killah-talks-returning-to-his-supreme-clientele-style (at the 5:00 mark, roughly) (accessed September 20, 2013). Admittedly, the Hieroglyphics logo is likely the second most tatted logo in hip-hop. *See* http://www.frank151.com/news/souls-of-mischiefs-still-infinity-tour-diary-week-three.html [pictures of fans with the Hieroglyphics logo tatted on them]. There is no accurate measure of which logo is tatted most, though.

[202] *See* http://www.hiphopdx.com/index/news/id.10721/title.allah-mathematics-readies-wu-massacre-recalls-wu-tang-clan-memories

[203] *See* http://youtu.be/sdOPu3TURA4 (accessed June 23, 2013). *See also* http://upload.wikimedia.org/wikipedia/en/thumb/c/c2/Wutangclanprotectyaneck.jpg/220px-Wutangclanprotectyaneck.jpg [an image of the original logo]

[204] *See* http://web.archive.org/web/20140303092958/http://www.wired.com/entertainment/music/magazine/15-11/pl_music [from the audio interview at the bottom of the page]

[205] *See* http://www.nytimes.com/1998/01/11/nyregion/new-yorkers-co-the-revolution-will-be-merchandised.html?pagewanted=2. Wu-Wear will be discussed in greater depth in the Addendum.

[206] *See* https://www.youtube.com/watch?v=11aXvISC9bA (accessed May 12, 2013)

[207] *See* https://www.youtube.com/watch?v=11aXvISC9bA (accessed May 12, 2013).

[208] *See id.* See also *The Wu-Tang Manual*, p. 43.

[209] See *The Wu-Tang Manual*, p. 48.

[210] See *Check the Technique: Liner Notes for Hip-Hop Junkies*, p. 450

[211] See *The Wu-Tang Manual*, p. 48.

[212] *See* http://youtu.be/1Z48HnRCXa0?t=5m5s [*U-God: Rise of a Fallen Soldier*]

[213] *See* http://youtu.be/1Z48HnRCXa0?t=4m57s. Curiously, Raekwon says he has known U-God since "third or fourth grade," also in the *U-God: Rise of a Fallen Soldier* documentary. It's possible that Raekwon forgot the two of them meeting earlier, at a younger age.

[214] Iconic group EPMD, for example, broke up when Erick Sermon (the "E" in the group name) discovered that Parrish Smith (the "P") was misappropriating group funds. In light of this, the MD in the group acronym (Making Dollars) seems sadly ironic *See* http://en.wikipedia.org /wiki/EPMD-First_breakup:_1993.E2.80.931996. *See also* http://www.youtube.com/watch?feature =player_detailpage&v=9y1Srz4S7fk#t=657

[215] *See* http://content.time.com/time/arts/article/ 0,8599,88545,00.html#ixzz2fVJx8Hq0. According to U-God, money from Wu recording budgets was even set aside for Ol' Dirty Bastard during his time in prison, although there is apparently a discrepancy regarding whether he ever received the money that was set aside for him. *See* http://youtu.be/1Z48HnRCXa0?t=8m44s

[216] *See* http://content.time.com/time/arts/article/ 0,8599,88545,00.html#ixzz2fVJx8Hq0

[217] *See* http://www.mvremix.com/urban/intervie ws/masta_killa_06.shtml

[218] *See id.*

[219] *See* Red Bull Music Academy interview, 2011.

[220] *See* http://allhiphop.com/2009/09/24/ghost face-wins-judgement-against-wu-tang-productions

[221] *See* http://www.rappersiknow.com/2009/01/28/this-is-an-amazing-interview-with-the-rza/ (accessed May 19, 2013)

[222] *See id.* In the aforementioned *Wildstyle Mag* interview, Rza speculated why he thought there had been an increase in litigation in the record business. "The music industry is plummeting real fast. So, as the industry plummets, what happens is that there [are] no deals being made. If there's no deals being made [for] rappers, what happens to the lawyers? They've got to close their firms, they can't make no money. How can they make money from the client now? Litigation! And that's why you will hear this coming up. Not only Wu-Tang, you'll hear it popping [up] throughout the industry. You'll hear somebody suing somebody, because there are lawyers advising to sue, so the lawyers can keep their [retainers]." *See id.*

[223] *See* http://www.law360.com/articles/264137/ghostface-killah-sues-umg-over-wu-tang-clan-roy alties

[224] *See* http://www.hiphopdx.com/index/news/id.6214/title.u-god-sues-wu-tang-music-group-for -170-000 (accessed July 13, 2013).

[225] *See* http://youtu.be/J2kWdW1fvRM (accessed July 11, 2013).

[226] *See* http://blogs.villagevoice.com/music/2013/07/u_god_rza_keynote_speaker.php (accessed July 24, 2013).

[227] *See* "Phantoms of the Hip Hopera" by RJ Smith, *Spin*, July 1997, p. 70. Closer to the present, however, Rza claims that the introduction of financial success and music business politics into the lives of the Clan has affected the group over time, even altering the spontaneous creativity that marked the group's (and the hip-hop genre's) heyday. "All the illest hip-hop from the 90s came from us hanging together and making songs with no money involved," Rza said. "I think that hip-hop [today], especially Wu-Tang hip-hop, is missing that. It's about coming through and dropping a verse with no price on it or real reason to do it other than making music. That's how a song like 'C.R.E.A.M.' got made. The day that was made, Method Man came to my studio to do a song—he only had lyrics and I had a beat. He kicked a verse a cappella, I dubbed it and played around with loops on an ASR keyboard while he rhymed…that raw element of hip-hop is missing." *See* http://www.laweekly.com/westcoastsound/2013/10/02/rza-headlines-la-weeklys-bedrocktoberfest-heres-our-interview.

Presumably, this session ended with Method Man just providing the hook on "C.R.E.A.M.," as I can find no source discussing a version of the song with a Method Man verse on it.

[228] *See* http://www.thedailyshow.com/watch/thu-march-24-2005/rza (accessed September 20, 2013)

[229] See *The Wu-Tang Manual*, pp. 46-47 [Rza's breakdown of the Supreme Alphabet].

[230] *See* http://www.blackapologetics.com/suprem ealpha.html.

[231] *See* http://www.blackapologetics.com/mathde tail.html

[232] In NGE, using God as a common noun is a way to refer to a black man, particularly one who has knowledge of NGE teachings (a/k/a "knowledge of self").

[233] Some listeners have argued that Ghostface was referring to getting a .40 caliber firearm to retaliate, but that doesn't fit the context of the story, where Ghostface sounds as if the shooting occurred right after he got his culture cipher (presumptively if he had a .40 caliber firearm on him, he would have fired back at the assailants himself instead of going back to recount the story to the Clan and get reinforcements).

[234] It is unclear who created this particular acronym/re-definition for Wu-Tang. Rza also referenced this acronym in an early Wu interview. *See* http://www.youtube.com/watch?feature=player_detailpage&v=YkoZY_-XG_c#t=386.

Longtime Wu-Affiliate and NGE adherent Cappadonna breaks down his entire stage name into the acronym Consider All Poor People Acceptable, Don't Oppress Nor Neglect Anyone. *See* http://youtu.be/bv3Q4-xO5bY?t=42s

[235] See *The Supreme Understanding: The Teachings of Islam in North America*, p. 119-120. Many Nation of Islam teachings were adopted by the NGE. *See* http://www.youtube.com/watch?v=1fWoINftahw

[236] *See* http://www.blackapologetics.com/fivepercentfaq.html

[237] *See* http://youtu.be/V0YWQk7l0hg?t=7m. When combining Supreme Mathematics concepts, gods use the phrase "all being born to" as the equivalent of an equal sign, following the addition of the first two Supreme Mathematics concepts. Thus, *knowledge* (1) [plus] *god* (7) *all being born to* [equals] *build and destroy* (8) or 1 + 7 = 8.

[238] See *The Five Percenters*, p. 182-183. According to this teaching, the lighter skinned babies would eventually come to comprise the white race.

[239] See *Spin* (February 1991), p. 76 [where Wise Intelligent and Lord Jamar break down how Yacub was chased to the Caucus Mountains]. *See also* http://en.wikipedia.org/wiki/Caucasus_Mountains

[240] See *The Wu-Tang Manual*, p. 32.

[241] *See* http://youtu.be/YkoZY_-XG_c?t=6m26s (*Wu: The Story of The Wu-Tang Clan*). Rza appears to have been in the studio working on *ETWT* when this segment was captured on film.

[242] There is a decent argument for a possible NGE influence on the title "C.R.E.A.M.." The first lesson in the 120 asks the question "Who is the Original Man?" and provides the answer "The Original Man is the Asiatic Blackman, the Maker, the Owner, the *cream* of the planet earth, Father of Civilization, God of the universe" [emphasis mine]. See *Women and New and Africana Religions*, by Lillian Ashcraft-Eason, Darnise Martin & Oyeronke Olademo (Praeger 2009), p. 45. See also *In the Name of Elijah Muhammad: Louis Farrakhan and The Nation of* Islam, p. 105. "Cream" being an otherwise unlikely metaphor for money, it is possible that Meth was metaphorically linking the priceless quality of godhood/black manhood with the value of money. Although other dairy products like "cheese" are also used as metaphors for money in hip-hop, whether those metaphors pre-date "cream" is another question.

[243] *See* http://comp.uark.edu/~tsweden/5per.html

[244] *See* http://www.babynology.com/meaning-jamel-m3.html

[245] *See* http://www.babynology.com/meaning-arief-m3.html

[246] *See* http://www.religionfacts.com/islam/places/medina.htm [explaining Medina's status as the second holiest city in Islam]. See *The Five Percenters*, p. 63 [explaining how Medina is the righteous name for Brooklyn in NGE]. *See also* http://www.metrolyrics.com/now-y-lyrics-la-the-darkman.html [referencing New York's righteous name in its title].

[247] See *Rappages*, February 1994, p. 45, "Wu-Tang Clan: 36 Chambers of Death...Choose One" by Cheo Coker. This part of the article can be read online at the following link: http://pressrewind.files.wordpress.com/2007/05/wutang_source2944.jpg. The 120 Lessons are also sometimes referred to as The 120 Degrees. *See* http://www.ancientorderoffreeasiatics.com/Mathematics.html. *See also* http://www.urb.com/2007/07/10/wu-tang-widdling-down-infinity/ [more discussion on numerology related to the Wu].

[248] *See* Red Bull Music Academy interview, 2011

[249] *See id.* [http://vimeo.com/30103392 at roughly 56:10]. This contradicts Rza's account, in *The Wu-*

Tang Manual, of being the first to expose Ghostface to knowledge of self.

[250] *See* http://vimeo.com/30103392

[251] *Id.*

[252] *See* http://allhiphop.com/2004/06/02/ghostface-change-gon%C2%92-come/

[253] *See* http://youtu.be/c_1xsQBgRTM

[254] *See* http://www.biblegateway.com/passage/?search=revelation%201:9-1:20&version =NIV

[255] *See* http://www.biblegateway.com/passage/?search=revelation%201:9-1:20&version =NIV

[256] See *Celebrating Sacraments* by Joseph Stoutzenburger, p. 78 (Saint Mary's Press 2000).

[257] See *Black Man's Religion: Can Christianity Be Afrocentric?* by Glen Usry and Craig S. Keener, p. 68 (IVP Academic 1996) ["Some modern Afrocentric writers point to the revelation of Jesus in Revelation 1:14-15 to claim that Jesus was Black, noting the hair like wool and feet like polished bronze."]. Years after *ETWT* was released, Rza would invite a producer/MC named Bronze Nazareth to join the Wu-Elements production team. *See* http://en.wikipedia.org/wiki/Bronze_Nazareth. Rza also makes several references to The Old Testament throughout his book, *The Tao of Wu*. See *The Tao of Wu*, pp. 7, 10, 205-206.

[258] *See* http://biblehub.com/matthew/5-39.htm

[259] *See* http://youtu.be/NdrTWoGwC7k

[260] *See* http://youtu.be/MZxgQJHbYqc?t=8m57s

[261] *See* http://youtu.be/Md83Lo0pfFc

[262] *See* http://www.geeksugar.com/GZA-Dark-Matter-30883619

[263] This is discussed at roughly the 25:45 mark of the audio interview with Gza found at http://www.geeksugar.com/GZA-Dark-Matter-30883 619 [the text of the message can be found at http://www.startalkradio.net/inspiring-the-next-generation/].

[264] See *Schooling Hip-Hop: Expanding Hip-Hop Based Education Across the Curriculum*, edited by Marc Lamont Hill, Emery Petchauer and Jeff Chang, p. 64, Note #1.

[265] *See* http://www.montrealgazette.com/Tang+Clan+followed+unlikely+path+McGill+lecture/9700882/story.html

[266] *See id.*

[267] *See* https://www.youtube.com/watch?v=11aXvISC9bA (near the 5:00 mark) (accessed May 12, 2013). Poppa Wu noted that Rza lived on the street that separated Stapleton from Park Hill and that Rza would literally lure in rivals from each project with music he played in his home, earning

him the nickname "The Pied Piper." *See* http://youtu.be/tjcjkRx6wHM?t=10m7s. See also *Wu: The Story of The Wu-Tang Clan.* In a voiceover, the narrator of the *Wu* documentary explained that Park Hill and Stapleton are only eight blocks from one another. The close proximity of the two housing projects made their conflict all the more deadly, as combatants could easily strike at a perceived rival and quickly retreat to their own projects.

[268] *See* http://www.thefader.com/2005/10/13/older-gods/ (dated October 13, 2005, accessed May 16, 2013) ["It was squashed before that, because brothers was always cool. The ones in Wu-Tang wasn't really warring with each other like that."]. The exact wording of Ghost's answer—as to whether the inter-neighborhood beef was squashed when Wu started—is somewhat open to interpretation since "like that" could mean some "warring" occurred, but not to a great degree (or that only a few members had any conflicts with one another).

[269] See *The Big Payback*, by Dan Charnas, p. 437.

[270] *See* http://www.thefader.com/2005/10/13/older-gods/

[271] *See* http://youtu.be/tjcjkRx6wHM?t=9m59s

[272] *See* http://articles.latimes.com/2012/nov/01/entertainment/la-et-ms-wutang-references-rza-iron-fists-20121101

[273] Red Bull Music Academy interview, 2011.

[274] *See id.* This chemistry was later revisited for Raekwon's solo debut, *Only Built 4 Cuban Linx*, where Raekwon and Ghostface shared vocal time for much of the album (and even were featured on the cover side by side).

[275] *See* https://www.youtube.com/watch?v=BWml7yoFwHA (accessed June 25, 2013)

[276] *See* http://halftimeonline.net/portfolio/inspectah-deck-wu-tang/ (accessed June 22, 2013).

[277] *See* http://www.allmusic.com/artist/inspectah-deck-mn0000770875/biography

[278] See *The Wu-Tang Manual*, p. 4.

[279] *See* http://youtu.be/1Z48HnRCXa0?t=4m7s

[280] *See* http://youtu.be/sdOPu3TURA4

[281] See *The Wu-Tang Manual*, p. 17. In an email exchange with the author, Will Strickland (shouted out in "Wu-Tang Clan Ain't Nuthin' To F' Wit") stated that Ol' Dirty Bastard's early role performing onstage alongside Rza involved being a dancer as well.

One can imagine this dance background had a similar influence on Dirty's critically acclaimed MC style. Strickland also noted that ODB could be seen dancing in the background of the video for The Genius' debut single "Come Do Me." *See* http://www.youtube.com/watch?feature=player_detailpage&v=ZTPB9inzOPU

[282] See *J. Dilla's Donuts* by Jordan Ferguson, p. 31 (Bloomsbury Academic 2014) [describing how copying the work of another hip-hop producer ("biting") is frowned upon and was once considered a "cardinal sin"]. Copying is frowned upon in hip-hop generally, across elements.

[283] *See* http://www.youtube.com/watch?v=D469kEb5VVA& (accessed June 24, 2013). This altercation is not the only clash that occurred between Clan members and other hip-hop acts, as album cover photography Daniel Hastings recalled one such incident between Wu and an unnamed veteran rap act which inspired the idea of having the Clan wear masks on *ETWT* album cover, as discussed in Chapter Five.

[284] *See* http://www.youtube.com/watch?v=Nx3xcDmJ9dE

[285] *See* http://www.youtube.com/watch?v=rt1PfIUMxRs&feature=player_detailpage#t=124 [Peter Rosenberg's "The Process" interview with Raekwon].

[286] *See* http://www.youtube.com/watch?v=rt1PfIUMxs&feature=player_detailpage#t=266 [Peter Rosenberg's "The Process" interview with Raekwon].

[287] *See* http://www.complex.com/music/2011/12/the-50-greatest-hip-hop-skits/wu-tang-clan-torture-skit

[288] *See* http://en.wikipedia.org/wiki/Good_Morning_Vietnam. Up to the time when *ETWT* was recorded, Vietnam was the longest running American military engagement. Wars in Afghanistan and Iraq have long since dwarfed Vietnam in both length and expense. For vintage footage of NGE adherents discussing their thoughts on the Vietnam War while it was still raging, *see* http://www.youtube.com/watch?v=-oOm7mSka0A

[289] *See* "Phantoms of the Hip Hopera" by RJ Smith, *Spin*, July 1997, p. 72.

[290] *See* http://massappeal.com/raekwon-peter-rosenberg-the-process/

[291] *See* http://www.xxlmag.com/news/2013/11/wu-tang-clan-members-revisit-enter-the-wu-tang-36-chambers/2/

[292] *See* http://grantland.com/features/wu-tang-clan-20th-anniversary-reunion-rza-gza-ghostface/

[293] *See* http://www.xxlmag.com/news/2013/11/wu-tang-clan-members-revisit-enter-the-wu-tang-36-chambers/2/

[294] See *Billboard*, April 2, 1994, p. 22, "The Rap Column," by Havelock Nelson. *See also* http://

www.nytimes.com/1994/05/15/nyregion/one-neighborhood-two-lives-special-report-death-staten-island-2-paths-cross.html?src=pm&pagewanted=1 [establishing Hawkins' age, as well as the date and location of the shooting].

[295] See *Billboard*, April 2, 1994, p. 22, "The Rap Column," by Havelock Nelson. Shyheim has suffered through numerous personal setbacks himself, including most recently turning himself in after he was suspected of committing a fatal hit-and-run on New Year's Day 2014. *See* http://gothamist.com/2014/01/08/wu-tang_hit_run.php

[296] See *Billboard*, April 2, 1994, p. 22, "The Rap Column," by Havelock Nelson

[297] *See* http://youtu.be/7m148vZDwJA?t=57s (accessed June 30, 2013)

[298] *See* http://youtu.be/7m148vZDwJA?t=4m26s (accessed June 30, 2013). *See also* http://tinyurl.com/kasemural [for a different angle of the mural, via Google Maps, partially obscured by a truck]. *See also* http://www.nytimes.com/1994/05/15/nyregion/one-neighborhood-two-lives-special-report-death-staten-island-2-paths-cross.html?src=pm&pagewanted=1 [discussing the murder of Kase, a/k/a Ernest Sayon, by NYPD officer Donald Brown].

While showing several European journalists the mural from the "Can It Be All So Simple" video,

Raekwon explained how several other names of deceased Clan affiliates were also added to the mural. *See* http://www.youtube.com/watch?v=QArQYzFqcDw

[299] See *Billboard*, April 2, 1994, p. 22. [Havelock Nelson's *The Rap Column* reporting that the album was certified gold, while C.R.E.A.M. is listed as #18 on the Hot Rap Singles chart on the same page, adjacent to *The Rap Column*].

As an indicator forecasting the forthcoming rise of Southern rap, "Player's Ball," the debut single from Outkast's first record was number one on the same chart.

[300] *See id.* at 25.

[301] *See id.* at 76.

[302] The difference in rankings of rap singles, depending on their coastal origin, in the aforementioned April 1994 Hot 100 *Billboard* chart goes well beyond the rankings of the Clan and Snoop and is likely illustrative of why some enmity arose on the East Coast (to which the West Coast inevitably responded). West Coast rap veteran Ice Cube sat at #38 on the same chart with "You Know How We Do It," while East Coast veteran Masta Ace's West Coast friendly ode to cars "Born To Roll" sat at #36. By contrast, traditional East Coast-sounding modest hits such as A Tribe Called Quest's "Electric Relaxation (Relax Yourself Girl)" and Queen

Latifah's "U.N.I.T.Y." were much lower on the same chart, at #65 and #69, respectively. Singles from East Coast veteran acts such as Gangstarr's "Mass Appeal" appear at #74 (in its 5th week [R.I.P Guru]) and Heavy D. and the Boyz "Got Me Waiting" appears at #77 (in its 2nd week [R.I.P. Heavy D]).

[303] Although Tupac Shakur was born and raised in New York City, his professional rap career began on the West Coast and he is considered a West Coast rapper.

[304] *See* http://www.avclub.com/articles/rza,13843/ (accessed June 25, 2013)

[305] *See* http://www.discogs.com/Prince-Rakeem-Ooh-I-Love-You-Rakeem/release/302116. Prince Paul apparently received no formal credit on the record, even though Rza personally credits Prince Paul with doing the drum programming on "Ooh I Love You, Raheem." *See* http://www.avclub.com/articles/rza,13843/

[306] *See* http://www.avclub.com/articles/rza,13843/ (accessed June 25, 2013). It's a bit unclear whether Rza's specific mention of "the high-hats" meant that Prince Paul only assisted with that part of the drum programming or if Paul programmed the drums alone. "He did the drums in it" implies the latter.

[307] Easy Mo Bee produced the B-side cut, "Sexcapades," which Rza co-produced. Rza

produced "Deadly Venoms." *See* http://www.discogs.com/Prince-Rakeem-Ooh-I-Love-You-Rakeem/release/302116

[308] *See* http://www.avclub.com/articles/rza,13843/ (accessed June 25, 2013)

[309] On that cut, Rza received co-production credit, while Easy Mo' Bee—who produced the majority of Gza's debut album on Cold Chillin'—was billed as the main producer.

[310] *See* http://www.discogs.com/Prince-Rakeem-Ooh-I-Love-You-Rakeem/release/302116

[311] See *Check The Technique*, p. 452.

[312] See *Check The Technique*, p. 452. Gza remains overlooked as a Cold Chillin' artist to this day. As of this writing, Gza is not even listed as an artist on the label's Wikipedia page. *See* http://en.wikipedia.org/wiki/Cold_Chillin%27_Records

[313] Despite both albums sharing extensive production input from Easy Mo' Bee, *Ready to Die* achieved much more commercial success than *Words from the Genius.* That success was ironically aided by the Clan's re-invigoration of the hardcore East Coast scene with *ETWT* the year before *Ready to Die* was released.

[314] *See* http://www.cnn.com/2009/SHOWBIZ/Music/10/12/rza.tao.wu.tang/

The shooting occurred in front of a building located at 160 Park Hill Road (an address to which Method Man often refers in Clan songs as "one six ooo"). This location figures prominently in Clan iconography, as the building where part of the "Protect Ya Neck" video was shot. *See id.*

[315] *See id.*

[316] *See* http://www.villagevoice.com/2000-05-23/news/wu-tang-clan-is-sumthing-ta-fuck-wit/full/

Rza beat the charge by convincing the jury of his claim of self-defense, in a case where he was accused of shooting another man named Willie Walters in the leg in Steubenville, Ohio (the town where Rza was born and to which he briefly returned to live before the Clan was formed). *See id.* Another less reputable source than the *Village Voice* claims the charge was attempted murder. *See* http://exclaim.ca/Features/Timeline/wu-tang_clan-days_of_wu. A third researcher, Alvin Blanco, also asserts that the charge was attempted murder, although he cites no source for his claim. See *The Wu-Tang Clan and Rza: A Trip Through Hip-Hop's 36 Chambers*, by Alvin Blanco, p. 8. A fourth researcher claims the charges were both attempted murder *and* felonious assault, also without citing a source. See *The Big Payback*, p. 436. A July 1997 *Rolling Stone* article on Wu wrongfully described Rza as being "acquitted of murder." *See* http://www.rollingstone.com/music/news/wu-tang-family-values-19970710.

[317] *See* http://www.cnn.com/2009/SHOWBIZ/Music/10/12/rza.tao.wu.tang/

[318] See *The Wu-Tang Clan and Rza: A Trip Through Hip-Hop's 36 Chambers*, p. 8. [briefly mentioning Ghost's Steubenville shooting incident]. *See also* http://www.complex.com/music/2013/03/how-21-rappers-responded-to-near-death-experiences/ghostface-killah. It has never been clear why Ghost was shot and I don't intend to speculate here.

[319] *See* http://youtu.be/MF6bjN9I4XE?t=2m27s

[320] *See* http://youtu.be/1Z48HnRCXa0?t=5m34s

[321] See *Check The Technique*, p. 453. U-God reflected in a separate interview that he had his first experience recording songs while in this group with Meth and Deck. *See* http://www.vice.com/read/the-wu-tang-clan-talks-obama-gay-rap-and-odb

[322] See *The Wu-Tang Manual*, p. 72. On Rza's debut single, he would feature three mixes of a B-side song entitled "Sexcapades." One of those B-side mixes was called The DMD Mix and another was called The DMD Radio Mix, both likely in tribute to the DMD crew formed by Meth, Raekwon and Deck. The third mix of "Sexcapades" was called The Wu-Tang Mix. *See* http://www.discogs.com/Prince-Rakeem-Ooh-I-Love-You-Rakeem/release/302116. Rza's brother 9th Prince remembers the crew being called "Dig Em Down." *See*

http://blogs.villagevoice.com/music/2010/10/ interview_9th_p.php.

[323] *See* http://nahright.com/news/the-green-room -with-u-god/ (accessed July 12, 2013). While it is unclear exactly when this show occurred, the context raises the inference that the group was performing to promote a physical record, thus the show likely occurred around the time of the re-release of "Protect Ya Neck" by Loud, since major labels traditionally finance promo tours (and it is doubtful that the group's *first* show would come as late as the release of *ETWT*). Contrast this with the early rap tradition of groups performing together extensively before they released records commercially, such as Grandmaster Flash and the Furious Five, who formed their group and performed extensively two years before they released a record. *See* http://en.wikipedia.org/wiki/Grandmaster_Flash _and_the_ Furious_Five

[324] *See* http://grantland.com/features/wu-tang-clan-20th-anniversary-reunion-rza-gza-ghostface/

[325] Red Bull Music Academy interview, 2011.

[326] *See* http://www.riotsound.com/hiphop/rap/ interviews/ Ugod-of-Wu-tang/index.php

[327] *See* http://www.vice.com/read/the-wu-tang-clan-talks-obama-gay-rap-and-odb

In a video interview, Rza recalled that Ol' Dirty Bastard's first experience rhyming onstage on Staten Island was losing a rap battle to Cappadonna. *See* http://youtu.be/11aXvISC9bA?t=9m36s (accessed May 12, 2013). Rza was careful to note, however, that Dirty was a Brooklyn resident at the time and Rza theorized that Cappadonna likely had the hometown advantage—as a Staten Island resident—when the battle was judged.

328 *See* http://en.wikipedia.org/wiki/Masta_Killa (accessed May 7, 2013) [citing as its source an interview on the DVD accompanying Masta Killa's *No Said Date* solo debut]. *See also* http://www.cracked.com/funny-6582-the-wu-tang-clan/

329 *See* http://www.youtube.com/watch?v=JE6HiVLzkyI (accessed July 14, 2013)

330 *See id.*

331 *See* http://www.xxlmag.com/features/2010/08/raekwon-the-making-of-only-built-for-cuban-linx/2/ (August 1, 2010 XXL article on the 15th anniversary of *Cuban Linx*). See also *The Wu-Tang Manual*, at p. 49 (sidebar).

332 *See* http://www.xxlmag.com/features/2010/08/raekwon-the-making-of-only-built-for-cuban-linx/2/ ["I was like two days out of prison," U-God recalled. "I just came out the penitentiary. I'd just come home on [Wu-Tang's debut album, *Enter the Wu-Tang*] *36 Chambers*, too. I did two

years in prison. I came home on parole–work release right before the first album was done. That's why I'm only on two songs on the first album. Then…I got violated for…eight more months."]

[333] *See* http://www.discogs.com/artist/191265-RNS.

[334] *See* http://skulltheft.tumblr.com/post/256038796/rza-on-gear (accessed July 13, 2013) (quoting Rza's as-told-to interview in a producer how-to column printed in the March 1995 issue of *Rappages*). That RNS was imprisoned can be inferred from Rza's usage of the euphemism that RNS had to "go away for a while."

[335] See *The Wu-Tang Manual*, p. 197. *ETWT* engineer Carlos Bess wrote in an online post that five songs on *ETWT* were produced on an EPS: "Bring Da Ruckus," "Wu-Tang Clan Ain't Nuthin' Ta F' Wit," "C.R.E.A.M.," "Protect Ya Neck" and "Tearz". *See* http://www.gearslutz.com/board/3926467-post23.html

[336] *See id.*

[337] See *Wu: The Story of Wu-Tang* (DVD extra, extended Raekwon interview)

[338] *See* https://www.youtube.com/watch?v=_BcJRnoGJeM #t=1523.

[339] *See* Red Bull Music Academy interview, 2011

[340] *See* http://www.avclub.com/articles/rza,13843/ (accessed June 25, 2013)

[341] *See* http://www.wudanggongfu.com/kungfu/visit.htm (accessed July 6, 2013)

[342] See *China Forever: The Shaw Brothers and Diasporic Cinema*, p. 232.

[343] *See* http://en.wikipedia.org/wiki/Wudang_Mountains [citing as a source: *Road Atlas of Hubei* (湖北省公路里程 地图册); *Hubei Sheng Gonglu Licheng Dituce* (中国地图 出版社 *Zhongguo Ditu Chubanshe*, 2007), p. 11 (Shiyan City), and the map of the Wudangshan world heritage area, on the back cover].

[344] *See* http://en.wikipedia.org/wiki/Wudang_Mountains

[345] *See* http://en.wikipedia.org/wiki/Stapleton,_Staten_Island (accessed May 13, 2013). Vanderbilt University was named after him.

[346] *Id.*

[347] Brooklyn was also the home of Masta Killa. *See* http://en.wikipedia.org/wiki/Masta_Killa

[348] *See* http://usatoday30.usatoday.com/news/nation/2011-08-03-New-Orleans-public-housing-rebuild-experiment_n.htm?csp=34news

[349] *See* http://youtu.be/FmQoqWWBKmU (accessed June 23, 2013)

---

[350] *See* http://en.wikipedia.org/wiki/Berta_A_Dreyfus_Intermediate_School_49. This school has also experienced its fair share of tragedy, such as a 2007 incident where a student had his spleen ruptured when textbooks were thrown at him. *See* http://www.silive.com/news/index.ssf/2012/09/staten_island_teen_settles_sui.html

[351] *See* http://en.wikipedia.org/wiki/Stapleton,_Staten_ Island (accessed May 13, 2013).

[352] "We were in Atlantic City and ran into Guru of Gang Starr. He was with this kid named Dan Smalls, who I used to work with at the Statue of Liberty. Guess who he's working for? Uptown Records. He's like, 'I've got a CD for you. It's the *Who's The Man?* soundtrack, but I want you to listen to my man. It's a single called 'Party & Bullshit',"' Meth recounted. "I listened to that shit, I was like, 'Ri-diculous. This nigga's insane!' But then I didn't hear nothing of it after that." *See* http://www.complex.com/music/2011/10/method-man-25-essential-songs/notorious-big-f-method-man-the-what-1994

[353] *See* http://youtu.be/XAs8HMg47e8?t=1m14s. The interviewer failed to ask Meth exactly what his job duties there entailed. Online media outlet *Grantland* reported that Meth worked at the souvenir stand during his time at the Statue of Liberty. *See* http://grantland.com/features/wu-tang-clan-20th-anniversary-reunion-rza-gza-ghostface/

In an interview with *Unkut*, Kool Kim (of Staten Island rap duo The UMCs) also recalled working at the Statue of Liberty with Method Man, alongside his fellow Clan compatriots U-God and Inspectah Deck, and the other half of The UMCs, Haas G. *See* http://www.unkut.com/2013/01/kool-kim-of-the-umcs-the-unkut-interview/

[354] *See* http://youtu.be/NdrTWoGwC7k.

[355] *See* http://youtu.be/NdrTWoGwC7k?t=1m19s

[356] *See* http://youtu.be/ccm-38AVktI?t=2m39s

[357] *See* http://youtu.be/hZ6Ha0p9ZUM?t=43s

[358] *See* http://youtu.be/Gmz9VTIPSNY?t=2m21s

[359] *See* http://youtu.be/1Z48HnRCXa0?t=24m28s. Unfortunately, U-God was arrested for drug possession and weapons possession before he could finish college. By the time he was released, Wu-Tang Clan was already in full motion. *See id.* It is unclear whether U-God ever returned to complete his degree.

[360] *See* "Phantoms of the Hip Hopera" by RJ Smith, *Spin*, July 1997, p. 74

[361] See *The Tao of Wu*, p. 10. Rza moved there because his own parents could not afford to take care of him in Stapleton.

[362] See *Spin*, July 1997, p. 74.

[363] See *The Tao of Wu*, p. 11-12.

[364] See *The Tao of Wu*, p. 14.

[365] *See* http://youtu.be/vtc19FwgbxE?t=6m20s

[366] *See* http://www.xlr8r.com/features/2008/09/rza-beyond-shaolin (accessed May 19, 2013)

[367] *See* http://www.xlr8r.com/features/2008/09/rza-beyond-shaolin

[368] Rza and Ghost's time in Steubenville was far from peaceful, however. As mentioned earlier, Ghostface was purportedly shot in the neck during their time there, while Rza would face criminal charges related to a separate incident. See *The Wu-Tang Clan and Rza: A Trip Through Hip-Hop's 36 Chambers*, p. 8. Steubenville is indeed sparsely populated, as the U.S. Census estimated in 2012 that the town had just 18,429 residents. *See* http://quickfacts.census.gov/qfd/states/39/3974608.html.

However, Steubenville is proportionately blacker than Staten Island, as the US Census estimated in 2012 that the black proportion of the population there was 15.9%. *See id.* Staten Island has a much larger population (468,730 people), but also a much whiter population, with non-Hispanic blacks equaling only 9.5% of its populace. *See* http://en.wikipedia.org/wiki/Demographics_of_Staten_Island

[369] *See* http://nahright.com/news/the-green-room-with-u-god/ (accessed July 12, 2013)

[370] In an interview with Smack DVD, one of Ghostface's associates recounted how the videos for "C.R.E.A.M." and "Can It Be So Simple" were both shot in the Stapleton Houses. *See* http://youtu.be/FmQoqWWBKmU

[371] *See* http://en.wikipedia.org/wiki/Clifton,_ Staten_Island.

[372] *See id.*

[373] *See id.*

[374] *See* http://www.silive.com/news/index.ssf/2007/12/students_set_record_straight_a.html

[375] *See* http://sabaink.wordpress.com/2009/10/13/killa-hill-new-documentary-from-acclaimed-filmmaker-gerald-%E2%80%9Cgee-bee%E2%80%9D-barclay-tackles-the-social-issues-of-urban-crime-violence/

[376] *See* http://www.nytimes.com/2006/11/17/sports/football/17bears.html

[377] *See* http://pulitzercenter.org/blog/untold-stories-killer-hill-liberia-civil-war-park-hill-staten-island

[378] *See* http://www.youtube.com/watch?v=QArQYzFqcDw

[379] See http://www.rollingstone.com/music/news /wu-tang-family-values-19970710

[380] Before Meth's debut, however, another oft-overlooked Wu-related album was released: *Six Feet Deep*, the debut album from Rza-affiliated group, The Gravediggaz. This album went gold. The group was comprised of Frukwan and Prince Paul of pioneering Brooklyn hip-hop band Stetsasonic, Rza and a fourth rap artist (now deceased) named Too Poetic. All the members in the group were signed to Tommy Boy Records at nearly the same time, in the Prince Rakeem era. Rza did not produce the Gravediggaz album, instead handing off production duties to Poetic and Frukwan, in addition to up and coming Wu-affiliated producers such as True Master and 4th Disciple (both of whom would later play a major role in producing the second Wu-Tang group album, *Wu-Tang Forever*).

[381] The "*mi casa*" line (meaning "my house" in Spanish) implicitly means you can't win in Method Man's home, either a sports analogy to home court advantage or a card game analogy to a player's inability to beat "the house" (the casino), depending on how you want to interpret the metaphor. Either reference reinforces the idea that Method Man's verbal dexterity is unbeatable by any potential opponent-in-rhyme. Iconic Latino MC Big Pun would later quote this line in one of his most lauded guest appearances, on Fat Joe's "John Blaze," which also sampled Method

Man for the hook. *See* http://rapgenius.com/Fat-joe-john-blaze-lyrics#note-2807756. Pun would reference the line again on the hook to his solo song "Wrong Ones." *See* http://youtu.be/06qGl8s9CyQ?t=27s

[382] *See* http://soundandthefoley.com/2013/04/30/a-tisket-a-tasket/

There was a hit cover version recorded by Ella Fitzgerald in 1938. *See* http://en.wikipedia.org/wiki/A-Tisket,_A-Tasket#cite_note-1

[383] *See* http://www.metrolyrics.com/disco-lady-lyrics-johnnie-taylor.html

[384] *See* https://www.youtube.com/watch?v=lbgao2keSjc. *See also* http://www.investopedia.com/financial-edge/1111/8-of-the-most-successful-ad-campaigns-of-all-time.aspx and http://articles.chicagotribune.com/1995-01-30/business/9501300009_1_bayer-consumer-care-bayer-aspirin-mcdonald. Just as likely, the 1988 *Shower to Shower* commercial with the ad tagline "Have you had your sprinkle today" may have inspired both the Meth line and the McDonald's tagline. *See* http://www.youtube.com/watch?v=FrchKZ3nNS4 (accessed May 11, 2013)

[385] *See* http://www.inlander.com/spokane/article-18342-mount-up.html (for LA-based writer Jeff Weiss' argument that Warren G saved Def Jam). In another interview, Warren G himself argued that he saved Def Jam, using specific

figures ("…when **Def Jam** was in a hole [in 1994] guess who saved 'em? **Warren G**. **Warren G** saved 'em. They made 100 million dollars [because of me]." [emphasis theirs]). *See* http://www.hiphopdx.com/index/interviews/id.1392/title.warren-g-the-g-code.

[386] *See* http://youtu.be/V0YWQk7l0hg?t=7m22s. True Master and 4th Disciple are credited with producing most of the album.

[387] *See Billboard*, p. 94 (August 19, 1995). Bone Thugs-N-Harmony were enjoying their second week at #1 in that same week.

[388] To see this theory at work, contrast the critical acclaim *Liquid Swords* received with the cooler critical reception for *Wu-Tang Forever*, the double CD the Clan released two years later, which was unfairly maligned by critics due to its length. While its intro was indeed overly long and its last three cuts were arguably the weakest on any Wu album, the rest of the *Forever* project contains some of the strongest Clan lyrics and production in their whole discography. Ironically, Gza's "half short, twice strong" line is from a track on *Wu-Tang Forever*, entitled "As High As Wu-Tang Get." The entire line goes "Yo, too many songs, weak rhymes that's mad long/Make it brief, Son, half short and twice strong."

[389] *See* http://www.nytimes.com/1998/01/11/nyregion/new-yorkers-co-the-revolution-will-be-merchandised.html?page wanted=2

[390] *See* http://www.nytimes.com/1998/01/11/nyregion/new-yorkers-co-the-revolution-will-be-merchandised.html?page wanted=2

[391] *See* http://www.complex.com/style/2011/10/wu-tang-forever-the-history-of-wu-wear/starting-off

[392] *See* http://www.complex.com/style/2011/10/wu-tang-forever-the-history-of-wu-wear/growth-of-wu-wear

[393] *See* http://www.complex.com/style/2011/10/wu-tang-forever-the-history-of-wu-wear/collaborations. *See also* http://sneakernews.com/2012/05/24/classics-revisited-wu-tang-x-nike-dunk-high-1999/

[394] See *Vibe* (November 2007), p. 52. This *Vibe Beat* story marking the 15th anniversary of *ETWT* also noted how *Wu-Tang: Shaolin Style* would inspire future first-person rapper games like *Def Jam Vendetta*, released four years later, in 2003.

[395] *See* http://www.nydailynews.com/archives/gossip/eve-2000-celebs-thinking-big-article-1.772429?pgno=1

[396] *See* http://www.avclub.com/articles/rza,13843/ (accessed June 25, 2013)

[397] *See* http://www.avclub.com/articles/rza,13843/ (accessed June 25, 2013)

[398] *See* http://www.avclub.com/articles/rza,13843/ (accessed June 25, 2013)

[399] *See* http://www.rwor.org/a/v19/920-29/925/rage.htm

[400] *See* http://www.avclub.com/articles/rza,13843/ (accessed June 25, 2013)

[401] *See* http://grantland.com/features/wu-tang-clan-20th-anniversary-reunion-rza-gza-ghostface/

[402] *See id.* The historical irony in that situation is that the Clan's "Method Man" single was one of the first hip-hop records added to rotation on Hot 97 and hip-hop is responsible for so much of the station's ratings success. One would think a few plane tickets would have been an easy request to grant, considering the role the Clan played in adding authenticity to their station when it initially switched to a hip-hop format.

[403] *See* http://www.redbullmusicacademy.com/magazine/crooklyn-dodgers-oral-history (accessed July 18, 2013)

[404] *See* http://slumz.boxden.com/f87/wu-tang-invades-hot-97-odb-mic-rza-1s-2s-june-1995-a-1978685/ (near the nine minute mark)

[405] Admittedly, there is some violence in the beginning of *Slam* and in the climax of *Bulsworth*.

It is easier to see why ODB participated in certain other soundtracks. ODB's contribution to the hip-hop film *8 Mile* makes sense, due to the depth of his own commitment to the art of battling specifically and hip-hop generally. The same logic applies to Ol' Dirty Bastard's decision to contribute to the soundtracks of hip-hop affiliated films such as *Belly* (co-starring Method Man) and *I Got The Hook Up* (starring rapper Master P). All three of these films contain their fair share of violence as well.

Finally, there was also no shortage of violence in the 2001 film *Bully*, another soundtrack to which ODB contributed. *See* http://www.imdb.com/title/tt0242193/?ref_=_15

[406] *See* http://www.dazeddigital.com/music/article/16679/1/dazed93-rzas-ghetto-symphonies

[407] *See* http://rapgenius.com/Ol-dirty-bastard-got-your-money-lyrics/f-b-i-don-t-you-be-watching-me?referent=F.B.I.%20don't%20you%20be%20watching%20me

[408] *See* http://www.thedailybeast.com/articles/2012/01/12/8-explosive-finds-in-wu-tang-clan-member-ol-dirty-bastard-s-fbi-files.html

[409] *See* http://www.villagevoice.com/content/printVersion/214422/. Unfortunately, the NYPD has a long history of shooting unarmed black men. Amadou Diallo and Sean Bell are two

prominent, relatively recent victims of this phenomenon.

410 *See* http://www.villagevoice.com/content/printVersion/214422/

411 *See* http://www.thedailybeast.com/articles/2012/01/12/8-explosive-finds-in-wu-tang-clan-member-ol-dirty-bastard-s-fbi-files.html

412 *See* http://www.thedailybeast.com/articles/2012/01/12/8-explosive-finds-in-wu-tang-clan-member-ol-dirty-bastard-s-fbi-files.html

413 See *The Great Rock Discography*, edited by Martin Charles Strong, p. 181 (Canongate U.S. 2004).

414 *See* http://www.mtv.com/news/articles/242/wu-tangs-ghostface-killah-pleads-guilty-attempted-robbery.jhtml

415 This type of plea arrangement, where defendants are threatened with an unbearably long prison sentence unless they plead guilty to a lesser charge to which they believe they are innocent, is common and largely explains the disproportionately large presence of black inmates in the U.S. prison population, since prosecutors have vast discretion to determine whether to make these type of unbalanced plea arrangements or to drop any filed charges altogether (prosecutors with racial animus often do the former for black defendants and the latter for white ones). Arguably, charges should have been

dropped in this case, a fight between equals, especially since the parking attendants allegedly were not wholly innocent. See *The New Jim Crow* by Michelle Alexander, for a larger discussion of how the criminal justice system unfairly targets black men.

[416] *See* http://watchmojo.com/video/id/11786/

[417] *See* http://youtu.be/MZxgQJHbYqc?t=1m57s (accessed September 8, 2013)

[418] Sadly, some projects announced in 2013 fell apart before they reached fruition. In September 2013, Rza's IMDB page said he had a biopic of famed Asian conqueror Genghis Khan in pre-production, but that information no longer appears there. *See* http://www.imdb.com/name/nm0753526/ (accessed September 8, 2013) (accessed a second time on December 27, 2013)

[419] *See* http://pitchfork.com/news/52169-rza-to-release-10-with-yoko-ono/

[420] *See* http://soultemplemusic.bandcamp.com/album/the-keynote-speaker. *See also* http://www.rollingstone.com/music/news/rza-on-his-new-movies-and-recording-with-paul-banks-20131008#ixzz2hLtCzZGT.

Interpol's debut album was released a scant four years after *ETWT*. *See* http://en.wikipedia.org/wiki/Interpol_(band)

[421] *See* http://www.billboard.com/articles/columns/pop-shop/5915731/faulkner-rza-ny-anthem-exclusive-song-premiere (accessed February 25, 2014).

[422] *See* http://youtu.be/7m_oE6DUxtM. That film has been plagued by some legal difficulties, as a November 2013 screening of the film scheduled to take place at the Brooklyn Academy of Music was stopped, due to a cease and desist letter sent by lawyers representing ODB's estate. *See* http://youtu.be/vtc19FwgbxE?t=5m19s.

Recently, Dirty's estate gave their permission for the film to be distributed. *See* http://www.hiphopdx.com/index/news/id.2625/title.ol-dirty-bastard-s-estate-authorizes-dirty-documentary-release

[423] *See* http://www.imdb.com/title/tt2322421/

[424] *See* http://www.youtube.com/watch?v=DR_y_IaLZXk. *See also* http://www.imdb.com/title/tt0990416/?ref_=nm_flmg_dr_1. The IMDB page has a 2007 release date listed, yet the trailer did not appear to debut until 2010. Whether the documentary will be released remains to be seen.

[425] *See* http://www.comedycentral.com/video-clips/tw2ltp/chappelle-s-show-wu-tang-financial. *See also* http://www.emmys.com/shows/chappelles-show to see the show's list of Emmy nominations (all of which it deserved to win). Near the same time as their *Chappelle's Show* appearance, Rza and Gza were also featured in

the 2003 film *Coffee and Cigarettes*, in a hysterical scene with Bill Murray outlining the dangers of caffeine.

[426] *See* http://www.hiphopdx.com/index/interviews/id.2221/title.inspectah-deck-confirms-lost-c-r-e-a-m-verse-wu-tang-reunion-album

[427] *See* http://www.xxlmag.com/news/2013/06/rza-to-see-de-la-soul-sampling-one-of-my-productions-it-gets-no-cooler-than-that/

[428] *See* http://en.wikipedia.org/wiki/Nothing_Was_the_Same#Singles. That social media strategy undoubtedly helped *Nothing Was The Same* go on to sell almost three quarters of a million records in its debut week.

[429] While the song itself says little about Wu-Tang, it is considered a tribute of sorts because of the title and the fact that Drake's song utilizes a vocal sample of the hook, and quotes some Raekwon lines, from "It's Yourz." *See also* http://www.youtube.com/watch?v=9OmS51lDEYg ["It's Yourz" video].

[430] *See* http://www.rollingstone.com/music/news/rza-on-his-new-movies-and-recording-with-paul-banks-20131008#ixzz2hLtCzZGT

[431] *See* http://www.xxlmag.com/news/2013/11/macklemore-reviews-wu-tang-clans-enter-wu-tang-36-chambers/

---

[432] *See* http://www.acclaimedmusic.net/Current/A890.htm

[433] See *101 Albums That Changed Popular Music*, by Chris-Smith, pp. 225-227 (Oxford University Press 2009).

[434] See *1001 Albums You Must Hear Before You Die: Revised and Updated Edition*, edited by Robert Dimery, p. 717 (Universe 2010).

[435] *See* http://consequenceofsound.net/2010/09/consequence-of-sounds-top-100-albums-ever/1/

[436] *See* http://www.ew.com/ew/article/0,,20207337,00.html

[437] *See* http://www.rocklistmusic.co.uk/steveparker/paulmorley.htm

[438] *See* http://web.archive.org/web/20130727084303/http://www.acclaimedmusic.net/Current/A890.htm. I added *The Source* to the list.

[439] *See* http://thimk.wordpress.com/2008/12/10/almost-classic-the-sources-45-micbroken-record-album-reviews-through-1995/

[440] Compilation albums and collections omitted; some indie releases omitted.

[441] The "C.R.E.A.M." single was certified gold in 2009.

[442] SRC stands for Street Records Corporation and represented the return of Steve Rifkind to the music industry, after Sony shut down Loud Records. *See* http://www.hollywoodreporter.com/news/steve-rifkind-loud-src-records-universal-akon-asher-roth-356394

[443] Not all films starring Wu members are included here; this is only a cross-section. Rza also composed the score for *Kill Bill Vol. 1* (2003), *Soul Plane* (2004) *Blade: Trinity* (2004). Asterisks indicate noteworthy appearances or appearances key to a film's plot.

[444] *See* http://www.flicksandbits.com/2014/02/24/us-trailer-unleashed-for-the-protector-2-starring-tony-jaa-rza-ratha-pho-ngam/65843/

[445] *See* http://www.imdb.com/title/tt3203616/?ref_=nm_flmg_act_3

16939922R00142

Made in the USA
Middletown, DE
28 December 2014